Reading through colour

Reading through colour

How coloured filters can reduce reading difficulty, eye strain, and headaches

ARNOLD WILKINS
University of Essex

WILEY

This publication is designed to provide accurate and authoritative information in regard to
the subject matter covered. It is sold on the understanding that the Publisher is not engaged
in rendering professional services. If professional advice or other expert assistance is
required, the services of a competent professional should be sought.

Other Wiley Editorial Offices

John Wiley & Sons Inc., 111 River Street, Hoboken, NJ 07030, USA

Jossey-Bass, 989 Market Street, San Francisco, CA 94103-1741, USA

Wiley-VCH Verlag GmbH, Boschstr. 12, D-69469 Weinheim, Germany

John Wiley & Sons Australia Ltd, 33 Park Road, Milton, Queensland 4064, Australia

John Wiley & Sons (Asia) Pte Ltd, 2 Clementi Loop #02-01, Jin Xing Distripark, Singapore
129809

John Wiley & Sons Canada Ltd, 22 Worcester Road, Etobicoke, Ontario, Canada M9W 1L1

Wiley also publishes its books in a variety of electronic formats. Some content that appears in
print may not be available in electronic books.

Library of Congress Cataloging-in-Publication Data

Wilkins, Arnold J.
   Reading through colour : how coloured filters can reduce reading
   difficulty, eye strain, and headaches / Arnold Wilkins.
     p. cm.
   Includes bibliographical references and index.
   ISBN 0-470-85115-5 (cloth : alk. paper) – ISBN 0-470-85116-3 (pbk. : alk. paper)
   1. Reading – Colour aids. I. Title.
   LB1050.27.W55 2003
   372.41 – dc21

                              2002155594

British Library Cataloguing in Publication Data

A catalogue record for this book is available from the British Library

ISBN 0-470-85115-5 (cloth)
ISBN 0-470-85116-3 (pbk)

Project management by Originator, Gt Yarmouth, Norfolk (typeset in 10/12pt Palatino)
Printed and bound in Great Britain by Biddles Ltd, Guildford and King's Lynn
This book is printed on acid-free paper responsibly manufactured from sustainable forestry
in which at least two trees are planted for each one used for paper production.

To the individuals who can benefit from coloured filters,
and to my family, Liz, Martha, Jonty,
and my parents, Barbara and Leslie,
and to my secretary, Avril,
and collaborators, Bruce and Liz,
and you!

"But soft, what light through yonder window breaks?"

Contents

About the author

Professor Wilkins obtained a doctorate from Sussex University for work on human memory. He then spent two years at the Montreal Neurological Institute (1972–1974) where he became interested in epilepsy. He returned to England to work as a research scientist at the Medical Research Council Applied Psychology Unit, Cambridge, from 1974 until the unit was disbanded in 1997, when he joined the University of Essex. He spent ten years studying the mechanisms of photosensitive epilepsy and techniques for treatment and this study broadened into more general interest in vision and health. He has been responsible for several innovations, including a clinical test of vision, the first controlled trial showing that fluorescent lighting is detrimental to health, the invention of the first scientifically designed system for ophthalmic tinting and its introduction into optometric practice. He has a wide range of research interests including the neuropsychology of vision, reading and colour, photosensitive epilepsy, migraine, typography, human memory, and attention. These interests have helped him formulate a unified theory of Visual Stress, detailed in a book with this title (Oxford University Press, 1995). He is currently head of the Visual Perception Unit at the University of Essex where he is co-ordinating research on the use of coloured filters in the treatment of reading difficulties and visual stress.

Acknowledgements

When the MRC system for Precision Tints was introduced into optometric practice in the UK in 1993, a reporting system was put in place so that any side effects or other untoward events could be recorded. There have been surprisingly few comments that have not been positive (less than 5%), and rather than identifying faults with the system, the comments have provided an interesting reflection on the benefits of this new form of treatment. At the suggestion of the publishers, I have included some of the comments throughout this book, where they illustrate the points I am making in each chapter. Rather than leave the punctuation and spellings unchanged and perhaps cause embarrassment, I have undertaken the usual editorial duties, and I have omitted the expressions of gratitude. I am grateful to the patients for permission to reproduce their comments. I am particularly grateful to Sam and his mother and to David and his mother for permission to reproduce their stories.

I would like to express my gratitude to the patients who have given their time willingly to participate in our research.

Many other individuals have been involved. They include Elizabeth Ashby, Peter Bex, Jenny Brown, Anne Busby, Edward Chronicle, Bruce Evans, Lyle Gray, Annette Grounds, Laura Hughes, Rebecca Jeanes, Anita Lightstone, Anne Maclachlan, Bundy Mackintosh, Judith Martin, Ian Nimmo-Smith, Tim Noakes, Regini Patel, David Pointon, Peter Pumfrey, Elizabeth Rowland, Avril Shelmerdine, Alex Shepherd, Anita Simmers, Fiona Smith, Nicola Stevenson, Rhonda Stone, Ruth Tyrrell, and Anne Wright.

I should particularly like to thank Bruce Evans and Liz Ashby (formerly Lewis) who have collaborated in many of the studies reported in this book. Liz has offered advice concerning the introduction of overlays into schools. Her work at the Norfolk Sensory Support Service, under the direction of David Pointon, has been responsible for setting the ball rolling in schools. Chapter 9 and the notes on classroom management are her work, and she contributed to the assessment using overlays, and the frequently asked questions sections.

Plates 1 and 2 were created using files from the web site of the Colour Group of Great Britain, courtesy of Dr Patrick Forsyth. The MRI image (Figure 5.2) is reproduced from the *Whole Brain Atlas* by Keith A. Johnson MD and J. Alex Becker (http://www.med.harvard.edu/AANLIB/cases/caseM/mr1_t/023.html) by kind permission of the authors. The areas of the visual cortex in the same figure are based on a graphic by George Mather PhD by kind permission.

I thank iOO Sales Ltd for permission to reproduce the material that appears in the Appendices.

Much of the research described in this book was conducted while I was a scientist at the Medical Research Council Applied Psychology Unit in Cambridge. I thank the director, Alan Baddeley, for giving me the freedom to investigate curiosities that appeared mere foolishness. The Applied Psychology Unit was the only institution of its kind in the world, and had a longstanding tradition of applying psychology to everyday problems, with a consequent development of psychological theory. Scientific traditions of this kind take time to develop and require a community of scientists with the appropriate informal interactions between individuals. I am not alone in thinking that the MRC administration made a sad and unfortunate error of judgment in disbanding the Unit and bringing the unique tradition to an end.

About this book

This book tells the story of the discovery and development of the use of coloured overlays and tinted glasses to help with reading, a simple intervention that can sometimes result in improvements that seem miraculous.

Overlays are sheets of specially coloured plastic suitable for placing over a page so as to colour the text beneath without interfering with its clarity. Their use in schools is becoming widespread because of the improvements in reading speed that the overlays can bring. In this book I explain exactly what overlays are and how to select them. I explain how tinted glasses differ from overlays, and review the scientific evidence as to how and why colour works.

Interspersed throughout are testimonies and comments in which children, parents, and teachers tell stories of how coloured filters have transformed their lives.

The science behind the use of coloured overlays and lenses is rather technical, but is confined mainly to Chapters 15 and 16. If you find these chapters heavy going, you can skip to the conclusion and move on to the next chapter.

Declaration

I am a scientist responsible for the development of the concept of visual stress as a neurological disorder, for the invention of the *Intuitive Colorimeter*, and for the design of the *Intuitive Overlays* and *Rate of Reading Test*. I receive an "Award to Inventors" at the discretion of the Medical Research Council, and this award is based upon sales of these products (but not sales of tinted lenses, for which the MRC receives no royalty). I do not have a financial interest in any other respect, and I am not involved in marketing. Although the methods described in this book are based upon my research, I have tried to give a fair and objective picture of the alternative systems available.

one

Prologue – Sam's story

"My name is Sam ____. I am now 14 years and 4 months old. This is my story.

"All my life I have been unable to see clear text.

"This is normal for me.

"I thought that everybody saw the same thing as me.

"I had to memorise everything that I wrote instead of going back and re-reading it.

"This was because I couldn't read my writing either.

"Nobody asked me if I had trouble reading or writing.

"I was kept in at playtimes and told to do lines.

"The older I got the harder writing became because I had to write more and more.

"I could not cope with the amount of writing.

"I felt let down and stupid because I couldn't do all the work that everyone else was doing easily.

"I gave up. I didn't know how to do the things that other people could do. I didn't know why.

"I was always exhausted when I came home from school.

"I often had headaches.

"This kept on happening to me until I had an eye exam that changed my life.

"I was due for an eye examination and went to a new optician.

"My mum told him that I was dyslexic and the optician offered a coloured overlay test.

"That test changed my life.

"I would never be the same again.

"The coloured overlay test came out positive!!!

"It was the most important moment of my life.

"For the first time in my life I could see text clear as glass.

"I was astounded.

"I looked at the page stunned.

"All I could think to say was 'How did it do that?'

"It was not easy to use the overlays because they made my headaches worse.

"Once I got my lenses the headaches disappeared.

"My life has been a lot easier because of them.

"Now my mum cannot stop me reading.

"I have become addicted to it.

"From being a person who refused to read I now plead with mum to take me to the library every weekend.

"I now feel happier and my self-confidence has increased."

Sam's mother continues the story

"Sam has always had good reports from school, but, from Reception, they always said that he could try harder with his writing. His teachers kept him in at playtimes to complete copying from the board, and I've lost track of the dinnertime playtimes he missed too, to complete work.

"His Primary School teachers always did their best for him, gave the extra support he obviously needed, and we worked closely together to support Sam, using the same strategies and practising skills. But, by the end of his primary school career, Sam was behind with his writing skills. He struggled to organise stories, couldn't decide what to put in reports, and his spelling was very strange, very phonic. No one could tell us what the hold-up was. Tests indicated he was between the high and low parameters, fairly normal, and nothing showed up. He sometimes had headaches and was always exhausted when he came home from school.

"I was sufficiently concerned about Sam's writing progress to visit his new High School and discuss this with his English teacher who was also Sam's form tutor. 'Don't worry,' he said. I asked for a syllabus or some curriculum notes per term, so I could work at home with Sam and support the particular things he would be working on. Nothing was sent home. We struggled.

"Year 7 parents' evening arrived. All Sam's teachers said they were happy with the progress he was making, but highlighted writing as a difficulty. They said Sam was lazy. In his End of Year 7 Report, every academic subject teacher noted that writing was something Sam struggled with. Avoidance tactics were also mentioned. I was concerned. Sam still had headaches and continued to be too tired to concentrate on homework.

"He came home from school one Thursday night, and said, 'My teacher said I'm dyslexic, but it's OK, I'm university material.' Sam is bright. I went to see the teacher who had tested my son and asked what kind of support he would get. 'Nothing,' she said. 'His scores aren't low enough to warrant intervention. Sam's lucky, he has a mum who's a teacher and knows how to help him.' I was to get terribly tired of hearing those words. I insisted that something be done.

"Sam had learning support for the rest of Year 8. He was taken out of English and Maths lessons for half of two lessons per week for a whole year. Homework was given out at the end of these lessons, and no one made sure Sam knew what the homework was. He got detentions for not handing it in. No information was sent home. We continued to struggle to support Sam with no focus.

"As a teacher myself, I believed that the tests Sam had had were correct in their diagnosis. They were. But they were not testing for the right thing. Conventional school testing does not show up all difficulties.

"I have done my share of hair-tearing, ranting in frustration, and shouting at him. I even told him – like his teachers – that he was bone idle and didn't want to work when he didn't want to do his homework. The rows were epic. Sam sometimes just looked at me. He believed every word I said to him. He didn't know any better, and neither did I.

"I became more concerned about the headaches, which sometimes were severe enough to make Sam distressed. He sometimes slept them off. I thought they were migraine.

"Year 9 dawned, and Sam received no support for his writing at all. I was a more frequent visitor to school, but nothing was done. That phrase, 'not low enough to warrant intervention ...' was used a lot. A little information and revision notes were sent home, but I still struggled to support Sam without curriculum focus on particular parts of the term.

"Easter 2001 arrived. Sam was overdue for an eye examination, so I booked him in with opticians new to us. I told them Sam was dyslexic, and they offered a coloured overlay test.

"It changed his life in seconds.

"Two weeks before his 14th birthday, Sam saw text on the whole page for the very first time. I have never seen a child so excited. He couldn't speak. It took his breath away. He said, 'Mum, is that what you see when you read? No wonder you can read so fast. I'm not thick. It's just like magic.'

3

"Sam brought the overlays home and left them in the kitchen on the worktop by the door, over an open book. He kept wandering into the room, looking at them, playing with them on and off the book, saying, 'I can't believe they do that' and shaking his head. We couldn't see it, the magic only worked for him. It took him a while to get used to using the overlays, but once he did he started to read more often, his confidence grew and then he couldn't stop. The headaches seemed to get more frequent.

"School were informed about the use of the overlays for reading only. His teachers were astounded when I told them about Sam's condition, but pleased that it had been discovered. Sam had to decide when to use them, but there was confusion. Teachers felt that he should be using them all the time.

"The overlays worked for reading Sam's own writing too. The first day he came home from school after the Easter holiday he said, 'Mum, my writing is appalling! My poor teachers, having to read that!' He had never seen a whole page of it before. There was a whole new world out there.

"Sam had the double green overlays for six weeks, then had lenses tinted dark green. The optician corrected a slight long-sightedness to compensate for the coloured lenses and to help stop the headaches. They have gone now. Sam uses the lenses at his discretion. The optician explained that if he felt he didn't need to wear them he didn't have to. Wrong use could damage his eyesight just like wrong use of any glasses (i.e., as sunglasses, for drawing, etc.), and sometimes he doesn't use them at all for short pieces of reading. Science and Maths are the two subjects we are often told he rarely wears his glasses in.

"He can copy from the blackboard properly now. He doesn't lose his place anymore and spends far less time finding where he is and more time working.

"Teachers still don't fully understand the implications and have no idea about visual stress; some teachers think he has to wear his glasses all the time, and still the school refuse to offer support for the dyslexia. They have, however, said they will reluctantly give him some educational psychologist time. We have had no other information about this to date.

"To be fair to them, I feel that they have never come across a child like Sam, and they are genuinely puzzled as to what to do about him. He is bright, and the difficulties he has along with their solutions are now being assimilated into the life of the school. It is a huge learning curve for all of us, but Sam will reap the benefits.

"As a special needs teacher myself, I had asked Sam what he could see when he read; all the usual questions I would ask my pupils ... 'Do the words jump about on the page, swim around, join together into one black blob, etc?' No, they didn't. I never asked if the whole page was a big blurry blob, though I wish I had, for that's what Sam sees when he looks at a page of text. He can focus on roughly three words at a time, and that's how he managed to slip through the net. Three words at a time were enough to hide the real difficulty.

"He never said anything because it was normal for him. He thought everyone could see the same as him, and he was just thick for not being able to read faster. It is testament to his hard work, intelligence, staying power, and use of coping strategies that he has made so much progress when he has had such limited vision for text.

"Sam continues to learn, he even does his homework willingly (some of the time!). And does he read? He now never stops. From not wanting to read at all, we now have to take his glasses away sometimes when we go to bed, because if he is reading an exciting book, he doesn't want to put it down.

"Now that's the real magic of coloured lenses, they're the doorway into a whole new magical world: one that never existed for Sam before."

two

In the beginning . . .

> ➤ How things began
> ➤ The pioneers, Olive Meares and Helen Irlen
> ➤ Innovation in coloured lens technology and the opportunity it offered
> ➤ A theory of visual stress
> ➤ The origins of the Intuitive Colorimeter
> ➤ The first masked clinical trials
> ➤ The Intuitive Overlays

In 1980 Olive Meares, a school teacher from Snell's Beach, New Zealand, published a paper in the journal *Visible Language* describing her pupils' reports of visual perceptual difficulties and how these difficulties could be reduced by covering the page with sheets of plastic, such as X-ray film, Perspex, etc. Three years later in 1983, Helen Irlen, a psychologist from California, read a paper to the American Psychological Association describing how her students reported fewer visual distortions when aided by coloured filters. In her book *Reading by the Colors* [1] she gives a description of how the discovery was made ...

> One day I was working with five students. One of the students had with her a red overlay she had used four years earlier in vision training exercises. Another student put the coloured sheet on the page she was looking at and gave a little scream. It was the first time she had ever been able to read without having the words constantly sway back and forth! Each of the other students tried to read with the red plastic sheet, but they found that it made no difference.

I decided to try other coloursheets as overlays to be placed on top of the printed page. We went to the theatre department and obtained as many different gels as they had available. Much experimenting with those coloured sheets showed an interesting thing. Of thirty-seven individuals with visual perception problems . . . thirty-one were helped by the coloured sheet. For each individual helped, certain colours could make things better but other colours could make things worse. But for each person helped, there was one colour that worked best.

Helen Irlen went on to experiment with coloured lenses. This was at the time when the advent of plastic lenses first made it possible to create coloured lenses cheaply and easily. Previously, it had been necessary to create a batch of glass, tinted to a particular colour, an expensive process that was justifiable only if a large number of lenses were to be made in that particular colour. Now, with plastic lenses it was possible to colour a spectacle lens by a different process. The lenses are usually made from a resin, allyl-diglycol-carbonate (known as CR39 because it was the 39th attempt on the part of the company that first made them, or so the story goes). The lenses can be coloured simply by dipping them into hot dye for a few minutes. The molecules of dye penetrate the surface and are held in the surface layer as the lens cools. By dipping resin lenses into a succession of dyes almost any desired colour can be obtained. Not only is this process far cheaper than tinting glass lenses, it has the further advantage that the coloration is independent of the thickness of the material, which is important with ophthalmic lenses. The technology had been used for cosmetic lenses, and Irlen decided to use it to see whether particular colours could be selected for her reading disabled clients. She made a set of trial lenses that could be combined to provide a range of colours, and discovered that she could often obtain a tint that clients found beneficial. She set up Irlen Institutes (subsequently Centres or Clinics, now in many countries), in which she licensed treatment with the coloured filters that she devised. Despite the anecdotal evidence for the success of her methods, her commercial activities aroused scepticism and ultimately the opposition of established practitioners of ophthalmic care, opposition which continues to this day in the USA. The Irlen diagnosticians are not trained optometrists, and the Irlen Centres remain outside mainstream optometric and ophthalmic practice. Although Helen Irlen has been criticised for "premature" commercialisation of her discovery, without her initiative and perseverance the discovery would have been submerged in a swamp of scepticism and might have sunk without trace. That being said, in order for a new treatment to make progress, we need to have scientific evidence that the treatment works, and ideally some idea as to why.

As a scientist with the Medical Research Council, I had spent 10 years researching photosensitive epilepsy; finding out precisely what it was about visual stimulation that was capable of inducing seizures in patients with epilepsy. I did this without actually provoking seizures, by using the electrical activity of the brain recorded from electrodes on the scalp, the so-called *electroencephalogram* (EEG). I discovered there were geometric visual patterns with very specific characteristics that enhanced the risk of seizures when these patients looked at them. Colleagues and friends would take one look at the patterns I used and say, "I could not look at that for long, it would give me a headache." They also reported a number of curious visual phenomena in the patterns: illusions of colour, shape, and motion. I discovered there were links between the illusions people reported and the headaches they had. For example, people who reported frequent headaches tended to report more illusions; the illusions tended to occur in the 24 hours before the start of a headache; and if the pain was on one side of the head the illusions tended to occur on one side of the pattern when you looked at its centre. Further experimentation revealed that as the characteristics of the patterns were altered, so the likelihood of illusions changed. It changed in exactly the same way as the likelihood of seizures in photosensitive patients! Particular patterns of stripes were the worst, the sort that the artist Bridget Riley uses to produce exciting visual effects. This led me to wonder whether the discomfort some people experience when they read might be due to the striped properties of printed text. I found that the illusions people reported in text were in fact remarkably similar to those reported in striped lines. When the "stripes" of text were reduced by covering the lines above and below those being read, the clarity of text improved, particularly for people who were susceptible to illusions in patterns of stripes. It was observations like these that led me to propose a neurological theory of visual discomfort. These developments are described in my book *Visual Stress* [2].

I was therefore intrigued when, in December 1985, the *Sunday Times* ran a report describing how the symptoms of visual stress could be treated with colour. I knew of early reports of coloured glasses, usually blue, being effective in reducing photosensitive seizures, and wondered if there could be a connection. I tried making an instrument that illuminated text with coloured light so as to study the patients who reported benefit from the Irlen filters. At first, I used three lamps, red, green, and blue. Almost any colour can be produced by mixing these three colours, in fact this is how a colour television works. I gave the patients controls that could change the brightness of the three lamps, but found that they had

8

Figure 2.1. Early versions of the *Intuitive Colorimeter*.

difficulty mixing the colours to produce the one they found helpful. The colour that you get is not the one you expect, for example, red and green combine to produce yellow. It was clear that I needed to change the instrument so that it was easier for patients to vary colours in a logical way. It was expensive and technically difficult to do this using a computer, and I tried to think of another way. One day I noticed the pool of light cast on the wall of my kitchen by a spotlight. I suddenly realised that by dividing the pool of light into a certain geometric configuration, colouring it, and then remixing it, it was possible to make the instrument I wanted. I could give the patients separate control over the three variables they intuitively understood: the colour (hue), the strength of colour (saturation), and the brightness. My employers, the Medical Research Council, patented the instrument. Later when the instrument was launched clinically I was asked to think of a name for it! The best name I could think of was Intuitive Colorimeter[1] (see Figure 2.1). I redesigned the instrument in 1999 to increase the similarity between the coloured light it provided and the light experienced when wearing lenses. The new design is described in Chapter 15.

I made the first few instruments in my garage, gradually improving the design from one model to the next. This was not without its hazards – beams of light can be hot, and one of the machines actually caught fire! I tried the instrument out in clinical practice, asking children with reading difficulties to look at text illuminated by coloured light while I varied the controls on the instrument. I was often able to find a particular colour that

---

[1] A colorimeter is a device that *measures* colour. A coloriser is a device that *produces* colour. The *Intuitive Colorimeter* is a coloriser, but, it is also a colorimeter in the sense that it measures the therapeutic tint. A machine interface is said to be intuitive, or intuitative, if it is easy to use. The Colorimeter is intuitive because the three subjective dimensions of hue, saturation, and brightness can be varied independently.

the children said stopped the distortions they normally saw. Initially I referred these children to the Irlen Centres, but there were many whose families could not afford to go. I tried using cosmetic tints to help these children. I remember them saying, "those lenses are good, but they are not as good as it was in the box" (referring to the Colorimeter). Before long I had heard this remark just once too often and decided to determine what it was that made the Colorimeter preferable to lenses that appeared to provide the same colour. This led me to realise just how precise the lens tint had to be. I had offered some blue lenses to a child who had selected a blue colour. It was only when the lenses exactly matched the colour in the Colorimeter that the child said that the lenses were as good as it was in the box. I remember my delight when she did so! With the help of Tim Noakes of Cerium Optical Products I had soon developed a set of tinted trial lenses that could very closely approximate any colour that could be obtained in the Colorimeter.

Early anecdotal successes were sometimes dramatic. One patient springs to mind. She was in her late teens but could not correctly read the words *was* and *saw*. In a list in which these words occurred at random her performance was similarly random. She was unaware of her errors, but reported that the *s* and *w* moved around. With a particular yellow hue this illusory movement ceased, and she was then able to read the words quite correctly, even though she was still unaware as to whether or not her performance was correct. Changing the hue slightly resulted in a return to the previous random performance.

Following publicity, we saw 50 individuals, mainly children, who reported perceptual distortions when reading. These volunteers were given coloured overlays, and, if the overlays were helpful, the volunteers were assessed with the *Intuitive Colorimeter* and offered lenses of the selected hue free of charge. We interviewed these individuals after they had been in possession of the lenses for more than 10 months. A surprisingly high proportion (82%) reported they were still using the glasses [3]. This provided the motivation and justification for a double-masked randomised controlled trial [4], which I will now describe.

If a patient believes in a medical treatment, the treatment will often be beneficial, even if it is medically quite ineffective. In order to assess any medical treatment scientifically it is necessary to control for these effects using a sham or dummy treatment. This is best done with a so-called double-masked randomised controlled trial in which the active treatment is compared with another sham treatment that is outwardly identical. To prevent the therapist inadvertently conveying his enthusiasm for the treatment, all participants, both the therapists and the patients, must be quite unaware which is the active treatment and which the sham, or *placebo* treatment. Both treatments are given out at random, using a code, and it is not until the end of the trial that the code is broken and patients know which treatment they received. No new drug is brought on to the market until it has undergone trials of this kind. These trials have many pitfalls. There is a story of a patient who proudly announced half way through a drug trial that the placebo pills were the ones that floated when she flushed them down the lavatory! This story illustrates not only the importance of matching the placebo and active treatments, but of ensuring the treatment is actually used! It had not been possible to evaluate the Irlen method using a double-masked trial because the individual being examined knew which colour of trial lens they found helpful during the assessment. They therefore might expect that colour to be helpful when lenses were offered in treatment. The individual's expectation, therefore, could contribute to, and confuse, any comparison of treatments.[2]

When individuals used the Colorimeter their eyes adapted to the colour, and they were usually surprised at how strongly coloured a spectacle lens appeared if it reproduced the chosen colour when the spectacles were worn under conventional (white) lighting. In other words, the appearance of the colour that reduced distortions in the Colorimeter could be separated from the appearance of the appropriate lens. This enabled a double-masked study to be undertaken because we were able to separate the colour that we knew to be effective from the colour appearance of the appropriate lens. I enlisted the help of two optometrists in this study, Dr. Bruce Evans and Mrs. Jenny Brown. Dr Evans had just completed a PhD on the subject of dyslexia at Aston University and, together with Dr Neville Drasdo, had reviewed the use of tints [7].

The children who took part in the study selected their optimal colour in the Colorimeter. The hue was gradually changed until the child reported the distortions starting to reappear, and this setting provided a sub-optimal placebo control. Spectacle lenses were made to match each setting, and one pair, active or control, selected at random, was glazed into frames and sent to the child. Of course, we could not be sure the control lens was actually inert, but we were fairly certain that the active lenses were more effective than the control. We asked the children and their parents to keep diaries in which they noted any symptoms of headache

---

[2] A scientific trial using the Irlen method has recently been reported but it is not clear whether it conforms to the strict criteria for a double-masked study. Using the Irlen method participants selected the optimal tinted lens and could therefore, at least in principle, remember their colour appearance when later given treatment. However, the investigators took care to provide the tinted glasses 3–4 weeks after the tint had been selected, and the sub-optimal placebo tints were "close" in colour [5, 6].

and eye strain and estimated how long each day the spectacles had been worn. Then the spectacles were returned and the frames were reglazed (active lenses being replaced by control and vice versa). The spectacles were then sent back to the participants for a second period of four weeks. There were fewer episodes of eye-strain and headache when the active lenses were worn than when the control lenses were worn, even though none of the study participants was able to distinguish between the two.

No trial is ever perfect. Many of the participants did not complete our study (it was, after all, quite a lengthy procedure), which means that our results were based on a slightly biased sample. A second problem was that it was possible that the placebo treatment was detrimental rather than inert, and that the differences we observed were a reflection of the detrimental effects of the placebo rather than the beneficial effects of the active lens. Nevertheless, the double-masked study lent support to the claims of beneficial effects, and convinced many in the optometric profession in the UK that coloured lenses could be helpful in reducing perceptual distortion. Up until then, most optometrists had been very sceptical. The study showed that the tint needed to be precise, and could be chosen using the *Intuitive Colorimeter*, and it justified our introduction of the *Colorimeter* into optometric practice. At that time, I was working for the Medical Research Council and they sold an exclusive marketing licence for the *Colorimeter* to Cerium Visual Technologies. The *Intuitive Colorimeter* has been in use in optometric practice in the UK for nearly ten years and clinical experience using the instrument has dispelled any remaining scepticism among optometrists.

We needed a simple way of identifying the individuals who might benefit from this new treatment, and of discovering the prevalence of visual stress in the general population. In 1994 I had collaborated with a teacher, Ruth Tyrrell [8], who used the Irlen techniques. We had shown that the Irlen overlays were effective at increasing reading speed following the earlier work of Greg Robinson in Australia [9]. Overlays are sheets of differently coloured plastic suitable for placing over a page of text when reading. Each child seemed to need a different colour. I measured the colours of the Irlen overlays and found that there was a range of shades that they omitted.[3] I therefore designed a set of overlays for use in research work (now sold as the *Intuitive Overlays*). The overlays sampled colour shades systematically and comprehensively, based upon applied colour science, as described in Chapter 7. These overlays proved effective at improving reading speed in several trials, most of which had placebo controls. The Medical Research Council sold an exclusive license for the

[3] The range of colours of the Irlen overlays was subsequently increased.

Intuitive Overlays to iOO Sales Ltd, a trading subsidiary of the Institute of Optometry, London. Cerium Visual Technologies, the company that markets the *Intuitive Colorimeter*, have since produced their own set of overlays based upon the *Intuitive Overlays*, but with slightly different characteristics.

In the study with Ruth Tyrrell, the increase in reading speed occurred only after 10 minutes continuous reading, when the eyes had become tired. In order to measure the effects of overlays on reading speed more quickly, I devised the *Rate of Reading Test* (see Chapter 8). The Medical Research Council sold a non-exclusive licence for the *Rate of Reading Test* to both iOO Sales Ltd and Cerium Visual Technologies.

Dr Bruce Evans and I have referred to the symptoms of perceptual distortion and associated benefit from colour as Meares–Irlen syndrome, in order to give credit to the people who made the initial discoveries. Other reports predate those of Meares and Irlen, but these authors provided the first detailed descriptions of large numbers of sufferers.

Although the methods described in this book owe their inception to the pioneering work of Meares and Irlen, they differ in important ways from the methods that Irlen herself developed. The techniques described in this book are based on applied colour science using two very simple assumptions, firstly that there are certain colours that are effective in improving fluency, and secondly that these differ from one individual to the next. These assumptions were justified at the time by clinical experience, although they now have empirical support. The assumptions meant that it was important to design a system in which any colour could be obtained with sufficient precision.

The assumptions were added to in 1999 when I redesigned the *Colorimeter* so that it gave not only the same colour but also the same mix of wavelengths as that provided by the lenses. This meant that people who are "colour blind" could use it. In Chapters 7 and 15 the tinting system and the assumptions underlying its design are described in more detail.

The *Intuitive Overlays* were launched in 1993 and are now in use in many schools. This book reviews the scientific evidence that coloured overlays can improve reading (Chapter 8), describes a simple method for determining whether overlays are likely to help (Chapters 10 and 11), and offers advice to teachers about classroom management (Chapter 12). The design of the *Intuitive Colorimeter* is described in Chapter 15 and the possible physiological mechanisms for the effects of colour on reading are reviewed in Chapter 16.

three

What is visual stress?

> The concept of visual stress
> Differences of interpretation
> Perceptual distortion is demonstrated and a list of possible distortions is given
> How to elicit symptoms from children
> Signs of visual stress and their specificity
> Meares–Irlen syndrome

When some people read, the page may seem too bright, their eyes may start to tire, and the letters may appear to move or blur. These symptoms are experienced by a surprisingly large proportion of school children (somewhere between 5 and 20%, depending on severity) and by a similar proportion of adults as well. The symptoms may indicate a condition of visual stress.

The term visual stress means different things to different people. Some divisions of the optometric profession ("behavioural optometrists") see it as the result of an imperfect functioning of the visual system, which their techniques are sufficient to correct. Sometimes, however, visual stress can occur despite perfect vision, and is closely related to photophobia (a dislike of bright light). In the previous chapter we saw how observations concerning photosensitive epilepsy led to the theory that visual stress can have a neurological basis. The symptoms and signs of visual stress can be a response to particular visual images, most notably, geometric patterns of stripes. According to the theory of visual stress, the brain is "overloaded" by certain images because nerve cells in the visual cortex of the brain fire too strongly and cause others to fire inappropriately. We will delve into these theories in Chapter 16. For now, let us consider the symptoms and signs of visual stress in more detail.

Symptoms of visual stress

The symptoms of visual stress usually include some aspect of perceptual distortion. If you are unaware of distortion when you read, look at the pattern in Plate 3 (page 150), which has been positioned at the end of this book for a good reason. If you suffer epilepsy or migraine DO NOT LOOK AT THIS FIGURE FOR MORE THAN A FEW SECONDS BECAUSE IT MIGHT INDUCE AN ATTACK.

If you look at the pattern you may experience distortions of the stripes, they may appear to move, to flicker or to blur, and faint colours may appear around or within the pattern. These distortions are sometimes called illusions [2, 10] and sometimes hallucinations [11]. Although their origin is not well understood, they provide clues as to the possible mechanisms of visual stress, as discussed in Chapter 16. Some of the illusions of movement may reflect the continuous variations in focus of the eyes, but others are more readily attributable to brain mechanisms, or more precisely, mechanisms whereby the brain controls the unwanted firing of cells (cortical inhibition) [2]. As described in the previous chapter, the individuals who experience distortions in Plate 3 are more likely than others to experience headaches and eye-strain [10], and there are many curious relationships between the nature of the headaches people suffer and the nature of the illusions they see. Individuals who report distortions in stripes are more likely than others to report distortions of text [12], perhaps because text is striped [2]. Many children report such distortions and their descriptions may be quite florid. When reading, the child may report:

▨ Movement of print – vibration, shifting side to side or up and down, words breaking up, words joining up, letters muddling, three-dimensional movement, movement of words around the word the individual is attending to, movement of words at the beginning and end of lines, and words "falling off" the page.
▨ Blurring print – closely spaced small print causes most problems. It is tempting to always attribute the blur to problems of focussing (accommodation), but blur can also occur as a result of problems that have nothing to do with the way the eyes focus.

░ Letters changing size.
░ Doubling of letters, extra letters appearing at the ends of words.
░ Letters fading or becoming darker.
░ Patterns appearing either in the dark print or in the white spaces. Sometimes these patterns are described as "worms", "rivers", or "waterfalls".
░ Illusions of colour – blobs of colour moving across the page, distracting the reader or obscuring words completely, or highlights of colour around letters or words (sometimes these extend to auras of light or rainbows around people and objects).
░ Nausea, dizziness, discomfort or even pain attributed to glare.

These reports are, of course, entirely subjective, and therefore difficult to verify. However, they tend to be consistent over time. If an individual complains of one symptom they are likely to complain of another in the list, although few individuals suffer from all the distortions.

One way of obtaining reports of symptoms of perceptual distortion is to ask open-ended questions such as, "When you read, do the letters do anything they should not do?" The above descriptions of symptoms have been obtained from questions of this kind. Questions such as these have the disadvantages that many individuals are unaware that the distortions they see are abnormal, and also, that individuals may feel under pressure to report symptoms unnecessarily.

Instead of asking questions that are open-ended and require memory, it may be preferable to ask questions with two or more definite alternative answers, and to ask these while the individual is actually looking at text. You might ask:

░ Do the letters stay still or do they move?
░ Are they clear or are they blurred (fuzzy)?
░ Are the words too close together or far enough apart?
░ Is the page too bright, not bright enough, or just about right?
░ Does it hurt your eyes to look at the print or is it OK?

These questions can help to identify the children who benefit from overlays, and the responses that indicate symptoms are those that suggest movement, blurring, running together of letters, glare, and eye or head pain. In general, the more of these symptoms that are reported the greater the increase in reading speed with a coloured overlay [13], see Chapter 8.

Symptoms are a subjective experience, and people differ in their awareness of such experiences, and their ability to describe them. An alternative way of evaluating visual stress is to observe what people actually do as they are reading, as described in the next section.

Signs of visual stress

Individuals may show physical signs of visual stress during reading. They may:

- move close to or away from the page and frequently change their head and body position;
- frequently look away from the page;
- yawn;
- track with their finger;
- rub their eyes;
- blink excessively or strangely;
- read slowly and haltingly.

In general, the people who suffer visual stress may show poor assimilation of reading content. They may tire quickly and the quality of their work may deteriorate rapidly. Concentration may be poor and attention span short. They may dislike reading and show reluctance to attempt literacy tasks. Often they have associated problems of frustration, low self-esteem, and behavioural difficulties.

There are varying degrees of severity of visual stress, and the number of signs and symptoms exhibited reflects this severity, at least in part. Unfortunately the signs and symptoms are not exclusive to visual stress, see Chapter 14. They can indicate difficulties with reading, which may be visual or more general. The symptoms and signs can be present in individuals with conventional problems of eyesight, such as refractive error (requiring glasses), difficulty adjusting focus, or a difficulty with co-ordination of the two eyes (binocular vision). The latter is usually treated with eye exercises, sometimes with glasses, and occasionally with surgery of the eye muscles. It is therefore essential that anyone who experiences the symptoms listed above or who has difficulty with reading obtains an examination from an optometrist or orthoptist, see Chapter 4. If they are asked to undertake eye exercises, these should be taken seriously.

If the symptoms and signs listed above persist despite ophthalmic treatment, there may be neurological mechanisms that underlie the visual stress, particularly if there is a family history of migraine. If this kind of visual stress is treatable with coloured filters, the symptoms and signs are referred to as Meares–Irlen syndrome. As will be shown in Chapter 8, the proportion of school children with Meares–Irlen syndrome is probably greater than 5%.

Meares–Irlen syndrome

As mentioned in the previous chapter, Olive Meares was one of the first to describe the symptoms and signs of visual stress among school children in her class. It was Helen Irlen, however, who first explored the benefit of coloured filters as treatment. She referred to the symptoms and signs as Scotopic Sensitivity Syndrome (SSS),[1] and later as Irlen syndrome, see Chapter 16. As we saw in the previous chapter, Bruce Evans and I introduced the term Meares–Irlen syndrome to give credit to both the pioneers.

Sometimes individuals who show dramatic improvements in reading fluency with a coloured overlay report no symptoms and show no signs of visual stress. They may even be fluent readers. Whether these individuals have Meares–Irlen syndrome is a question of definition. There is, as yet, no 100% reliable way of knowing whether an individual will find an overlay helpful for reading other than by examining them with overlays and the *Rate of Reading Test* as described in Chapter 10.

Tired eyes and optometry

Tired eyes and headaches are common among school children [8, 13–15]. The school eye examinations that used to be commonplace have largely been discontinued. There are many visual difficulties other than short or long sightedness, particularly problems of binocular co-ordination, and, without a visit to the optometrist, these problems can go unnoticed, even though they may be interfering with schoolwork and responsible for headaches and eye strain. Many children never go to see

---

[1] This was rather an unfortunate term because it increased the scepticism among vision scientists. The word scotopic comes from the Greek $\sigma\chi o\tau o\varsigma$, which means darkness, and it is used to refer to twilight vision when the sensitive rod photoreceptors are active, see Chapters 5 and 6. The rods are not responsible for colour vision, and there is as yet no evidence for their selective involvement in the syndrome.

---

an optometrist. Those that do and are prescribed "eye exercises", may not be diligent in carrying them out, and, if glasses are prescribed, they are not always worn.

It is, therefore, up to parents and teachers to be aware of the visual difficulties children can have, and to see that children are referred to an optometrist if there is any suspicion of visual problems. It would be wise for any child that benefits from an overlay to have an optometric examination.

About 20% of the school population have problems that require an optometric examination according to Thomson and colleagues who have developed software that allows teachers to screen their children for visual problems [16]. The identification of pupils who require optometric examination is important in its own right, but will not help identify those individuals who benefit from overlays, because there is little correlation between benefit from overlays and the results of conventional optometric and orthoptic examinations.

Conclusion

Visual stress is a condition that affects reading, making the perception of letters and words tiring, and discouraging reading. The visual stress may reflect conventional eye problems requiring treatment, but it can persist in the absence of any such difficulties. When it does, there is often migraine in the family. Often the symptoms of visual stress can be treated using coloured filters. The symptoms of visual stress that remit with coloured filters are sometimes referred to as Meares–Irlen syndrome, and sometimes as Irlen syndrome or scotopic sensitivity syndrome.

four

Professionals responsible for eye care and vision: a guide for parents

➤ Optometrists (ophthalmic opticians)
➤ The eye examination
➤ Dispensing opticians
➤ Orthoptists and binocular vision
➤ Ophthalmologists, school nurses and doctors
➤ School psychologists

Readers who are unfamiliar with the various specialties involved in caring for sight may find the following summary helpful.

Opticians are the most numerous vision specialty. There are two groups of people who are commonly called opticians: optometrists and dispensing opticians. Optometrists measure visual function, check the appearance of the back of the eye (fundus), check the pressure within the eye, determine the strength of lens that best corrects any error of refraction, and advise on exercises that may be necessary to correct disorders of binocular co-ordination. Optometrists were previously known in the UK as ophthalmic opticians but now prefer the American term "optometrist" to help distinguish their activities from those of the dispensing optician. The dispensing optician measures the patient for frames, orders the lenses and frames suitable for the patient, and helps to fit them. Both optometrists and dispensing opticians are involved in contact lens practice.

Some optometrists work in hospital ophthalmology departments, but most work from community practices in town centres. In the UK these practices are increasingly owned by large business concerns, and these organisations place corporate constraints on the way in which individual optometrists work. Many optometrists have special interests, and some concern themselves particularly with how the eyes work together. There is not always sufficient time for optometrists to follow their special interests during the conventional eye examination.

Binocular vision is also the specialty of orthoptists. Orthoptists usually work from hospital ophthalmology departments, and are usually concerned with children's vision, particularly squint and disorders of binocular co-ordination. Orthoptists work under the direction of ophthalmologists. Ophthalmologists are surgeons who specialise in disorders and diseases of the eye and eye muscles.

School nurses and school doctors have been involved in screening children's vision, although it has to be said that the techniques at their disposal are often insufficient to reveal clinically significant problems – problems that can be responsible for scholastic underachievement. In some cases the school eye test can be counter-productive: it can give parents a false sense of security when visual problems go undetected.

Among the rarer specialties involving eye care are neuro-ophthalmologists, who specialise in nervous diseases of the eye, eye muscles, and visual pathways. They often call on the skills of clinical electrophysiologists who measure the electrical activity of the body such as that from the eye and the visual part of the brain. Research psychologists, physicists and psychophysicists are also involved in measuring visual function, but teachers and parents are unlikely to encounter these individuals. They may, however, come across school psychologists, also known as educational psychologists. These individuals are not trained to measure visual function, although visual perception is within their remit. Some are familiar with Meares–Irlen syndrome.

In addition to the above professionals, each education authority has a group of teachers with special qualifications in visual impairment, responsible for helping partially sighted children.

Routes of referral

Patients can refer themselves to optometrists, but the referral to other medical vision specialists usually begins with a letter from a General Practitioner. For an orthoptic assessment, patients are usually referred to a hospital eye department, although in a few regions orthoptists are involved in school screening. When it comes to issues concerning exam dispensation, schools now have procedures for obtaining advice from appropriately qualified specialist teachers or psychologists who can then complete a request for consideration by the examination board. The regulations are frequently reviewed.

five

The eye and visual pathways

> The eye
> Magnocellular and parvocellular pathways
> Visual areas of the cortex

The complexity of the visual pathways and brain areas is such that it is difficult to know how and where the benefit from overlays arises. Some of the arguments addressed later in this book therefore require a little knowledge of the structure of the eye and the visual pathways. The following is a brief summary.

The eye is shown in cross section in Figure 5.1. An image of the world is brought to focus on the curved surface at the back of the eye. This surface is called the *retina*. The focusing is done mainly by the curved surface of the front of the eye, the *cornea*, but also by the internal lens. The shaping of this lens is controlled by muscles, making it possible to achieve the best image on the retina (thin shape for a distant object, fat shape for near). The image is upside down, but this is of no consequence, given the way the brain analyses the image. The retina consists of a mosaic of light-sensitive cells of various types (see Chapter 6).

Light-sensitive cells convert light to electrical and chemical signals that are transmitted via the optic nerve to various areas of the brain. Most of the visual information is fed to a relay station near the centre of the brain, known as the lateral geniculate nucleus, and then onwards to the visual cortex at the back of the brain. This pathway is known as the geniculo-striate pathway, see Figure 5.2.

Different parts of the brain specialise in different aspects of vision. The geniculo-striate pathway is wired so that images to the left of the centre of

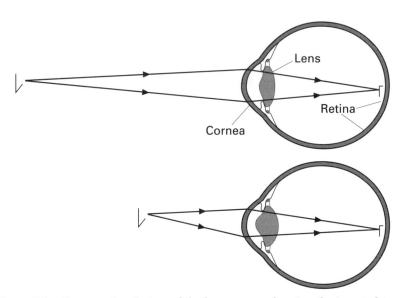

Figure 5.1. Cross-sectional view of the human eye, showing the inverted image formed on the retina by the cornea and lens, and the way in which the lens changes shape in order to bring a near object into focus on the retina.

gaze are analysed in the right half of the brain (cerebral hemisphere), and vice versa. The pathway is divided into two main subpathways. One, the magnocellular pathway, has the large cells in two layers of the lateral geniculate nucleus, and the other, the parvocellular pathway, the small cells in the remaining layers. The magnocellular pathway has fewer neurons but is responsible for the rapid detection of changes in the visual scene. The parvocellular pathway is responsible for the slower analysis of stable detail. We will encounter these pathways again in Chapter 16 where we discuss the magnocellular deficit theory of dyslexia.

There are various visual areas of the cortex, each with different functions. For example, in one area called V5, the cells are principally responsive to movement of the image on the retina; in another area, V4, the cells respond to colour. The approximate position of these visual areas is shown in the far right panel of Figure 5.2.

Although most of the visual information is fed to the visual cortex, it is worth remembering that there are several other pathways, some of which control eye movements.

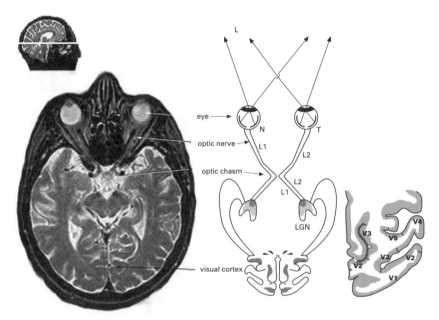

Figure 5.2. (Left) Magnetic resonance image of the human brain shown in horizontal section at the level given in the profile, top left. (Right) Diagram of the visual pathways. Objects to the left of the centre of gaze L are imaged on the nasal half of the retina of the left eye N and the temporal half retina of the right eye T and relayed via the crossing pathways of the optic nerve L1 and the non crossing pathways L2 to the lateral geniculate nucleus (LGN) in the right cerebral hemisphere. They are then relayed to the visual cortex at the back of the head. This is shown magnified, far right, with some of the visual areas labelled. The areas are contiguous, but the slice appears to divide them (reproduced by permission of Keith A. Johnson and J. Alex Becker, © 1995–1999, *Whole Brain Atlas* [http://www.med.harvard.edu/AANLIB/cases/caseM/mr1_t/023.html]).

six

Why we see the world in colour

> ➤ The nature of light
> ➤ How colour is perceived
> ➤ Colour blindness and Meares–Irlen syndrome
> ➤ Representing colours on a map

As we saw in the previous chapter, light is brought to focus by the eye onto the retina. On the retina are light sensitive cells called photoreceptors. The photoreceptors are divided into those called rods and cones on the basis of their shape. Light reception is not confined to rod and cone photoreceptors [17], but these are the receptors responsible for vision. The rods enable us to see in starlight and the cones are used exclusively for daylight vision. The rods are more sensitive than cones, but provide only fuzzy vision because groups are wired together to improve their sensitivity. There are three types of cones, each type exhibiting different sensitivity to different wavelengths of light.

Visible light consists of electromagnetic radiation similar to radio waves, but very much shorter in wavelength. The wavelength of light is so small that it is measured in nanometres, or "nm", with one thousand million nanometers in a single metre. The visual spectrum includes wavelengths in the range 380 to 780 nm. If roughly similar energy is present at all wavelengths throughout this range we see white light, but when the energy is greater at some wavelengths than others the light appears coloured. When the light has a narrow range of wavelengths the colour is strongly saturated. For example, light appears red if it has energy only at the long-wavelength end of the visible spectrum (above about 600 nm). Light with energy only at the short-wavelength end (below about 450 nm)

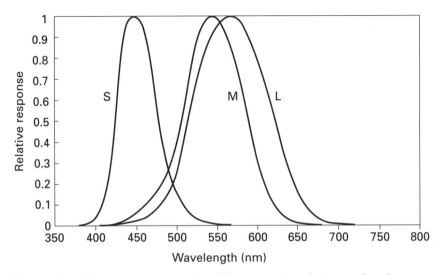

Figure 6.1. The spectral sensitivity of the cones: S – short-wavelength cones, M – middle-wavelength cones, L – long-wavelength cones (based on data from reference [18]).

appears a deep blue. Light with energy mainly at middle wavelengths may appear yellow or green depending on precisely where the energy is at a maximum.

Each of the three types of cone photoreceptor responds differently to light according to its wavelength. The long-wavelength sensitive cones, L-cones for short, are most sensitive to light at wavelengths of about 565 nm, but will respond to light over most of the visible range, albeit to a lesser extent. The second class of cones is known as the middle-wavelength, or M-cones. M-cones are most sensitive to light at wavelengths of about 545 nm, but also have a very broad range of sensitivity, which overlaps considerably with that of the L-cones. There are relatively few short-wavelength, or S-cones, and they respond mainly to wavelengths in the range 410–505 nm with a peak sensitivity at 445 nm, see Figure 6.1.

The range of sensitivity of the cones is so broad that most coloured light that we experience will stimulate all three classes of cones. It is the relative stimulation of these three classes of cones that is used by the brain to determine the colour we see.

We see the colours in a rainbow because light rays with different wavelength are bent differently by raindrops to reveal the colours of the spectrum, shown in the graph in Plate 1 (lower left). But we can see more colours than simply those that appear in the spectrum. Purple is one example. Purple is usually perceived if light has more energy at both the short and at the long-wavelength end of the spectrum than in the middle. Both the long-wavelength sensitive cones and the short-wavelength cones then respond more than the middle-wavelength cones.

In some individuals, about 8% of men and 0.5% of women,[1] one class of cones is missing or dysfunctional. The individuals are commonly said to be colour-blind although this is a misnomer. Colours can be experienced, but some colours are confused with others. The proportion of individuals with Meares–Irlen syndrome who have a colour vision anomaly seems to be just the same as in the population at large [19, 20]. This suggests Meares–Irlen syndrome is nothing to do with anomalous colour vision.

The most common forms of colour anomalies give rise to a confusion of red and green. This confusion is often detected using the Ishihara Test [21]. The test requires the recognition of numbers made up of a collection of coloured dots mixed with dots of a different, but confusable colour. All the dots vary in brightness, but the numbers stand out provided red is not confused with green. Unfortunately a few individuals with Meares–Irlen syndrome fail this test. They fail it not because of a confusion of reds and greens but because the glare generated by the high contrast between the dots and the background makes it difficult for them to pick out the numbers. As a result, they are told they have a colour vision problem when they do not, and this can have unfortunate consequences because some careers are closed to those who are colour-blind (e.g. pilots). Colour vision anomalies can be assessed using different tests that involve the discrimination of shades of colour (for example, the City University Test [22]), and these are more suitable for individuals with Meares–Irlen syndrome.

Representing colours on a "map"

We are all familiar with paint charts and the curious names that are given to subtle shades in an attempt to identify and discriminate them. These charts do not do justice to the fact that colours vary on a continuum. For our purposes it will be necessary to represent colours on a map that allows for the continuum of shades. Maps can be complicated because a flat surface is often used to represent a surface that has three dimensions. Colours exist in three dimensions. If you are thinking at the physiological

[1] The proportion depends on region. These figures are for the UK.

level you can conceive of these dimensions as the energy captured by L-, M- and S-cones. If you are thinking in terms of colour sensation you can conceive of the dimensions as hue (colour), saturation (strength of colour), and brightness.[2] Either way, any point in the three dimensional space is determined by the outputs of the three classes of cone.

Just as the world is often more conveniently represented by a map than by a globe, so it is often more convenient to represent the three dimensions of colour on the two dimensions of a map. This is done by keeping one dimension constant or undefined, and this dimension is usually brightness. The colours on the map of colours therefore usually represent all the colours you can see at a given brightness.

One of the most widely used colour maps is the Uniform Chromaticity Scale (UCS) diagram from the Commission Internationale de l'Eclairage (International Lighting Commission, CIE) [23]. Any colour that you can see is represented by a point somewhere on this diagram. Plate 1 (central image) provides an approximation (it is not possible to represent the diagram perfectly because printing techniques do not provide a sufficiently large range of colours). White is near the centre and will appear grey because an attempt has been made to keep the brightness of all the colours similar.

There are many different shades of white, but the white that occurs when all the wavelengths throughout the spectrum have the same energy is given by the coordinates $u' = 0.210$, $v' = 0.474$. These coordinates specify a colour in exactly the same way as latitude and longitude specify a location on the earth's surface. Find the white point on the map in Plate 1 by locating 0.210 on the horizontal axis and then move up the map until you are level with 0.474 on the vertical axis. The further a point is from white the stronger, i.e. the more saturated, is the colour. The curved edge of the diagram shows the colours of the rainbow, and these *spectral* colours are the most saturated you can see. (They do not appear saturated when we look at the rainbow because they are mixed with other light from the sky.)

The advantage of the diagram is that the distance from one point to another is roughly proportional to the ease with which the two colours represented by the points can be discriminated.

It is important to appreciate that the position on the map, known as the *chromaticity*, is a physical quantity. Given the physical measurement of the

---

[2] Note that saturation and brightness often vary together when you are mixing pigments, strongly saturated colours usually being rather dark. In principle, however, saturation is quite independent of brightness, as will be familiar to readers who have used photoediting software.

energy at each wavelength, it is possible to calculate the chromaticity of any light or surface, and therefore place the colour in the appropriate position on the map. The chromaticity gives an approximation to the perceived colour. Provided the proportion of light energy captured by the three types of cone is the same, the chromaticity will be the same. Once you know the chromaticity, you know the relative stimulation of the three classes of cone.

There are very many different ways of combining the energy at each wavelength in order to achieve the same stimulation of the cones and the same chromaticity. There is therefore a many-to-one correspondence between the distribution of energy across the spectrum and the chromaticity associated with this distribution.

Unlike chromaticity, colour is not a physical quantity—it is a subjective sensation. Although chromaticity is a physical approximation to the psychological sensation, colour appearance depends not simply on chromaticity but also to some extent on the viewing conditions.

One of the best-known maps of the world, the Mercator projection, shows longitude as vertical lines and latitude as horizontal. Although this is the most widely used projection of the world, the shortest path between two points (a great circle) is not a line but a curve on this projection. For some purposes it is preferable to use a different projection (Gnomic projection) in which the shortest path is represented as a straight line. No one projection is suitable for all purposes. It is the same with maps of colour. No map is suitable for all purposes. An alternative colour map was proposed by MacLeod and Boynton [24] in which the difference between the L- and M-cones provided one axis of the map. You can think of this as a red–green continuum. The other axis was a blue–yellow continuum derived from the the the S-cones. This projection is suitable for representing the way in which the signals from the cones are combined and opposed. You can appreciate colour opponency by looking at a strongly coloured surface for a minute or two, and then at a white or grey surface. You will experience an afterimage that is of opposite (complementary) colour. This suggests that the visual system is processing colours by opposing the outputs of the cones in some way. The Macleod–Boynton diagram helps with the study of this opponency.

In any map of the world, a given point on the map determines a position on the earth's surface. This is the case for all projections. The same is true in maps of colour. In both the Macleod–Boynton and CIE UCS colour maps [23] the position of a point determines the relative stimulation of the three classes of cones. One map can be translated into the other by a simple process.

As mentioned earlier, the design of the overlays was based on two simple assumptions: (1) that there are certain colours that are effective in improving fluency, and (2) that these effective colours differ from one individual to the next. Given these assumptions, if one wishes to maximise the chances of selecting the optimal colour, it is important to be able to sample colours systematically and comprehensively. The CIE UCS diagram represents colours in such a way that equal distances on the diagram represent roughly equal perceptual differences between colours [23]. Therefore, it was possible to use the CIE UCS diagram to select a series of chromaticities for the overlays that would provide a comprehensive and systematic colour choice. At the time, the physiological mechanisms underlying the benefits of overlays were unknown, and no further assumptions could be used to guide the design. As it has turned out, the assumptions are probably sufficient.

Having found out about Meares–Irlen by accident I decided to get my daughter Sarah assessed. The first tests showed a dramatic improvement in Sarah's ability to read using filters. I have never heard Sarah read with fluency, comprehension, and an understanding which up 'till the test had been unachievable. I have worked closely with teachers at her school and in the last few months (including the period since receiving her glasses) she has grown in confidence. Academically she has shown huge improvement. She participates far more willingly, she concentrates, she is happy to read aloud (now at twice the speed), she is starting to enjoy books, she has shown a steep improvement in her maths, English, and science.

Mother of 11-year-old girl

It's like seeing the world again. I can see as others have seen for all of their lives. I finally can pick up a book and read it like everyone else. I don't need to be scared of reading anymore.

17-year-old woman

The tinted glasses have made a tremendous difference to my son. His hand-writing and written work have changed almost beyond recognition, and, since having the overlay previously, his reading has improved dramatically. This has increased his confidence enormously and he is far, far happier at school.

Parent of 8-year-old boy

seven

What are coloured overlays?

> ➤ Technical details of the *Intuitive Overlays*
> ➤ The reasons behind their design

Coloured overlays are sheets of coloured plastic designed to be placed over a page of text. They colour the page beneath without interfering with the clarity of the text. The overlays can improve reading fluency in some people, but, as we will see in Chapter 8, the colour has to be selected to suit each individual. The overlays are therefore sold to teachers and eye care professionals in Assessment Packs, which include a wide range of colours. The overlays can be placed one on top of another so as to create an even wider range of stronger colours.

There are several types of overlays on the market. The *Intuitive Overlays*[1] have been used in the greatest number of research studies and are described below. The Assessment Pack includes nine differently coloured overlays and one grey overlay. The Cerium Overlays[2] are similarly designed but with a slightly different set of colours.

As mentioned in the previous section, the overlays are designed to sample colours as comprehensively as possible given the number of overlays, providing as close an approximation to any particular colour as possible. This is achieved in a similar manner to paints in a paint box.

---

[1] The *Intuitive Overlays* are sold by iOO Sales Ltd, a marketing subsidiary of the Institute of Optometry, London, a charity. The address is 56–62 Newington Causeway, London SE1 6DS, UK.
[2] The Cerium Overlays are sold by Cerium Visual Technologies Ltd, Cerium Technology Park, Tenterden, Kent TN30 7DE, UK.

Although there may be relatively few pigments in the paint box, they can be combined to produce a wide range of colours. So it is with the overlays: a wide range of colours can be produced by combining the overlays, placing one upon another. You can think of the overlays as providing a pallet of colours.

Technical details concerning the *Intuitive Overlays*

The overlays have colours represented by the points on the map shown in Plate 1 (central image). The map is the CIE UCS diagram referred to in the previous sections [23].[3] The inner ring of circular white points shows the chromaticities of the nine coloured overlays. The outer ring shows the chromaticities of double overlays: two overlays, one superimposed upon another. The resulting colours are darker and stronger (more saturated). Although it is quite possible to place any one overlay on top of any other, it is only necessary to combine the overlays as shown in the outer ring of Plate 1 (central image) in order to sample colours systematically. The grey points in the outer ring show the chromaticities formed by two identical overlays superimposed. The grey points are connected by single lines to the white points to indicate the overlays that were superimposed to obtain this colour. The crosses show the chromaticities of double overlays formed from overlays of different, but neighbouring chromaticity. The crosses are connected by lines to two white points to indicate the component overlays. To make this clearer, the necessary colours are shown by verbal description in the pie chart in Figure 7.1.

As explained in the previous chapter, the central diagram in Plate 1 (central image) encloses points representing all the colours that we can see (ignoring their brightness). The point near the centre represents white, the white that we see when light has the same energy at all wavelengths.[4]

---

[3] The printed colours are only a crude guide to the colours represented by the diagram because it is technically impossible to print the most saturated colours around the edge of the diagram.

[4] Because the diagram takes no account of brightness, the chromaticity of the grey overlay is the same as that of white. If we wanted to take account of brightness we would do so by means of a third dimension rising from the page. The chromaticity of white would then be directly above that of the grey overlay. But for now, let's keep things simple.

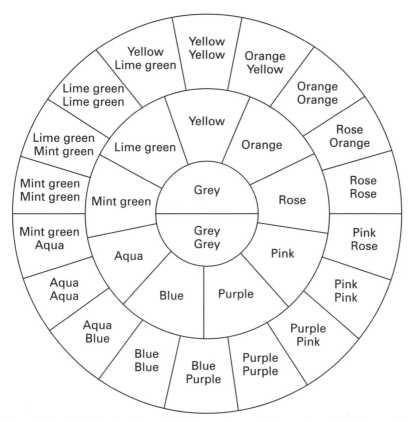

Figure 7.1. A circle of colours. Neighbours have similar colour. Double overlays are shown in the outer ring.

The points representing the colours of the single overlays and double overlays cluster evenly around white. This means that colour is sampled systematically and comprehensively. It is not possible to produce any colour with the overlays, but the difference between the colour required and the colour available will never be greater than half the distance between the points. This corresponds to only about 5 times the colour difference that can just be discriminated by the human eye.

The brightness of surfaces covered by the overlays are not shown in Plate 1. They are measured in terms of the amount of light the overlays reflect when in contact with a white surface (*reflectance*). These measurements are adjusted for the overall sensitivity of the eye (*photopic luminance*). The reflectances are between 48% and 79% for all the colours except yellow (90%). For double overlays the reflectances vary between 24% and 68%, with the exception of double yellow (80%).

It will be obvious from the figure that there is a large range of colours that lie outside the outer ring of points. Stronger colours outside the outer ring are available, but only by adding three or more overlays together. In practice this results in combinations that are dark. The filters take away light, and it is not possible to obtain a really strong colour without the combination of filters being dark.[5]

The overlays have a matt coating on one side and are gloss on the other. The matt surface reduces reflections of light sources from the surface of the overlay, but it has the disadvantage that it reduces the clarity of the text beneath slightly. The clarity is improved when the gloss surface is uppermost and the matt surface is in contact with the page, but this is practical only if surface reflections of room lights and windows can be sufficiently reduced. In practice this is possible when the room has few lamps and windows and the light from them comes in one direction. Provided surface reflections are avoided, the reduction of contrast is a matter of a few percent and the colour does not vary much with the angle of viewing.

Note that because of the matt surface, the overlays must be used in contact with the page. They cannot be held close to the eyes or used away from the page. This is an important aspect of design. When filters are used close to the eyes (as coloured spectacles) the optimal colour differs, see Chapter 15.

Figure 7.2 shows how the chromaticities of light reflected from the overlays vary under different types of lighting. Notice how the range of chromaticities available changes. Under daylight there is a good range. This range is somewhat curtailed under fluorescent light, particularly for blues (lower left), and the chromaticities are sampled slightly less evenly. Under the light of a filament lamp, which has very little energy at the short-wavelength end of the spectrum these differences are exaggerated. If the eyes are adapted to the illuminating light, as is usually the case, the changes due to lighting are allowed for by brain mechanisms[6] and the colours appear either the same or similar. Whether these mechanisms apply when colour influences reading speed has not yet been explored.

[5] Some people can tolerate the darkness and benefit from combinations of three overlays, but for most individuals who need a strong colour, coloured lenses or coloured lamps may provide a more practical solution. The provision of the appropriate colour in lenses and lamps is a complex issue which we will postpone until the *Intuitive Colorimeter* is discussed in Chapter 15.

[6] Those that underlie adaptation and colour constancy.

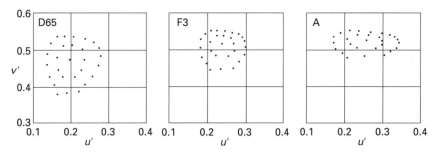

Figure 7.2. The chromaticities of light reflected from the *Inituitive Overlays* under three types of lighting: left panel, daylight (CIE Type D65); centre panel "white" (halophosphate) fluorescent lighting (CIE Type F3); and right panel, incandescent light from a filament lamp (CIE Type A) [23].

It was to avoid complications of this kind that I developed the *Intuitive Colorimeter*, and studied the effects of changing the colour of lighting (which is similar to the effects of wearing tinted glasses). These complications will be considered further in Chapter 16. For now, it is important to note: (1) the range of chromaticities is large with all types of lighting, and (2) the choice of overlay under lighting of one type may not be appropriate when the lighting is changed. It is therefore important to assess the effects of overlays with lighting under which the overlays will be used.

The *Intuitive Overlays* are supplied in a Teacher's Assessment Pack. The pack includes two A5 sized overlays of each of the following colours: rose, orange, yellow, lime green, mint green, aqua, blue, purple, pink and grey. A more exact description of the colours is given by their chromaticities shown in Plate 1 (central image). The pack also includes textual stimulus material and instructions for use. Cerium Visual Technologies also produce a pack of overlays similar to the *Intuitive Overlays*. The overlays supplied by the Irlen Institute do not sample chromaticity systematically, and are often restricted to members of Irlen's organisation.

eight

How do we know that coloured overlays work?

> ➤ Overlays can reduce fatigue and increase reading speed in at least 5% of the school population
> ➤ A new test of reading, the *Rate of Reading Test*, helps with the assessment of overlays
> ➤ Overlay choice is not simply due to suggestibility or motivation
> ➤ Skilled readers are not necessarily those who read more quickly
> ➤ The design of text in children's books is suboptimal

It is now known that coloured overlays can reduce the symptoms of visual stress, including headaches from reading, and they can improve reading speed. When these extraordinary assertions were first made by Helen Irlen [25], they were met with widespread scepticism, justified at the time by the lack of scientific evidence to substantiate the claims. Over the years supportive evidence has gradually accumulated. Alternative explanations in terms of increased motivation or other placebo effects have been eroded, and overlays are becoming an accepted reading aid.

Much of the early research remains unpublished, perhaps partly because it was of poor scientific design, as reviewed elsewhere [7]. To show that coloured overlays or tinted glasses provide a real advantage, any scientific study needs to demonstrate that the apparent benefits of overlays are not simply due to the effects of practice or changes in motivation. There are several ways of doing this, and most have been tried, as we will see. For instance, to ensure that practice is not distorting the results we can test some individuals with a coloured overlay first, and then without, and we can test other individuals in the opposite order. This ensures that any overall improvements with the overlay cannot be due to practice. To check for effects of motivation we can include a clear overlay, which could not affect reading except by influencing expectation or motivation. These precautions were taken in a study by Tyrrell and colleagues [8]. They selected reading material that was suitable for the children's reading level from the school library and photocopied passages for later use. The children then chose the most suitable colour of overlay. They did so by comparing the clarity of a page of text covered in turn by different overlays, including the clear overlay and seven others of various colours. About half the children chose the clear overlay as best; the remainder chose one of the coloured overlays. The children were asked to read the photocopied passages on two sessions, three weeks apart. The children read with the chosen overlay on one of the sessions (chosen at random) and without the overlay on the other session. In each test the reading continued for 15 minutes. Reading speed was measured by counting the number of syllables read in each minute. At the start of each reading session there was no difference in speed between the two conditions, i.e. with and without an overlay. Differences emerged only after the children had been reading for 10 minutes and had begun to tire. The children who had chosen a coloured overlay slowed down when they were reading without it, and reported symptoms of visual stress. The children who had chosen a clear overlay, on the other hand, reported fewer symptoms, did not slow down, and showed no difference in reading speed with the clear or the coloured overlay. The findings tend to suggest that it was the children who chose coloured overlays who were more subject to fatigue from prolonged reading, and that, for whatever reason, this fatigue was reduced when coloured overlays were used.

The above study used the Irlen overlays because they were the only overlays available at the time. The chromaticities of the various possible combinations of these overlays were measured and it was found that there were areas of the colour map that the overlays did not sample. With financial help from iOO Sales and a generous benefactor, the *Intuitive Overlays* were developed, as described in the previous chapter.

The newly developed *Intuitive Overlays* were then used in several small-scale studies in local authority primary schools [14]. About 50% of children in these mainstream schools reported beneficial perceptual effects with use of one or more of the overlays. These children were all given their best overlay to use if they wished to do so, and 3 months later nearly half the children who were given overlays were still using them: that is about 20% of the entire sample of normal school children. The children who used their overlays had slightly poorer reading skills. Effects of motivation and so on, the so-called placebo effects, tend to decrease over time, so the fact that so many children continued to use their overlays for so long tends to suggest that the benefits were real. Of course, children tend to conform, and it is quite possible that some used their overlays despite the inconvenience involved simply because others were doing so. This difficulty of interpretation was addressed in a different way, as we will see.

In the research by Tyrrell and colleagues [8] the effects of overlays on reading speed were observable only after 10 minutes continuous reading when the child had begun to tire. The reading speed was quite variable, and depended on how well the child understood the story they were reading as well as how clearly they could see the text. Any improvements in reading speed due to the overlay might require a long period of reading in order to be measurable simply because of variability in how well they understood the story. We obviously needed a test of reading speed that was less variable and would show up the effects of the overlays more quickly. We therefore designed a different type of reading test, now known as the *Rate of Reading Test*. The test consists of a passage of text that does not make sense! It consists of 10 lines, each with the same 15 common words in a different random order. The words are familiar to poor readers who are therefore prepared to undertake the challenge of reading. The random word order ensures that no word can be guessed from the context; each word must be seen to be read. The absence of any meaning has the advantage that children are often unaware of their errors of omission and transposition of words. The text is printed in a small typeface, closely spaced, in order to increase the visual difficulty. It is read aloud as quickly as possible for one minute. The score is the number of words correctly read.

The task of reading randomly ordered common words is quite bizarre, but it is simple and fun for children to undertake and it has turned out to provide a sensitive measure of the visual skills involved in reading. Provided individuals have been given the chance to experience the task once, and are therefore familiar with its demands, they do not improve their reading speed appreciably with further practice at the task, even when re-reading identical passages. This is a useful feature of the test because it needs to be given twice, once with the chosen overlay and once without, in order to compare the reading speed under the two conditions. Several studies have now shown that the reading rate is greater with the overlay in those children who will subsequently use the overlay voluntarily in the long-term [13, 14, 26]. The increase in reading speed is not simply due to more careless reading because, in general, if children read more quickly with an overlay, they also read more accurately [26].

Recent versions of the test have included a greater number of lines because a few fast readers finished the passage within the minute.

Placebo effects

It was useful to find a measure of reading speed that quickly showed the benefits of an overlay, but how could we be sure that the improvements in speed were not simply a reflection of changes in motivation? One could argue that clear overlays are not an adequate control for the motivating effects of a pretty coloured overlay. To answer these issues more directly we used motivational instructions. Reading rate was compared with no overlay, the chosen overlay, a grey overlay, and a grey overlay that was identical except that it carried the label "scientific prototype". The children were told that the prototype was new, that it combined all the colours, that they were one of the first children to use it, and that they were expected to do as well as they could. Performance with this grey overlay did not differ from that with the other grey overlay, although reading with the chosen coloured overlay was superior [15]. Bouldoukian had earlier used a similar research design, with similar results [27]. It would seem that the beneficial effects of overlays are not simply a reflection of motivation.

In the next chapter, which is a case history, we show that the increase in speed with an overlay can be greater when the text is small and closely spaced than when the text is large and widely spaced. If the increase were simply the result of motivation, one might not expect this difference.

Ultimately there is no perfectly satisfactory way of ensuring that the increase in reading speed is more than a placebo effect other than by means of a study with a double-masked design. As we saw in Chapter 2 this is a research design in which neither the person carrying out the test, nor the person being tested knows which intervention is the one that should produce an improvement. Such a study is not possible with overlays because the beneficial colour is chosen by the individual and can subsequently be recognised. As described in Chapter 2, however, such a study is not only possible with lenses, but has actually been carried out. The study showed fewer symptoms of eye strain and headache with the active tint than with the placebo. Unfortunately, the study was conducted before the *Rate of Reading Test* was available.

An even more convincing argument against the placebo effect explanations comes from the discovery of an objective abnormality in those who benefit from tints. The abnormality concerns the focusing of the eyes, and will be described in Chapter 16.

Non-optimal colours

If some colours are good for reading, are other colours bad? This question was addressed in a study by Jeanes and colleagues [14]. The *Rate of Reading Test* was given in five conditions: without an overlay, with a clear (transparent) overlay, with the Grey overlay from the set of Intuitive Overlays, and with two coloured overlays from the same set, one of the chosen colour and one of a colour opposite (complementary) to that chosen. The five conditions were presented in random order to allow for any effects of practice. With the overlay of the chosen colour, the reading rate was superior to that with no overlay, that with a clear overlay and that with the Grey overlay. The reading rate with the overlay of complementary colour was not different from the rate in the other conditions. In other words the complementary colour did not make reading worse than that with no overlay, but neither did it make it better.

In another study [15], children undertook the *Rate of Reading Test* with no overlay, an overlay that was reported as having least benefit, the Grey overlay from the *Intuitive Overlays* (50% reflectance), and the chosen overlay. The four conditions were presented in random order. The reading rate increased in the order in which the conditions are listed above, although the only difference that could not be interpreted as simply due to chance variation was in the performance with the chosen overlay *vis-à-vis* the other conditions. In other words, the chosen overlay was best for reading, but the worst overlay did not make a difference.

The effects of colour were compared with those of brightness in a further study [13] in which children used overlays. Some of the children chose the Grey overlay which they did not continue to use, and which had no effect on their reading speed.

The above studies are therefore consistent in finding: (1) that coloured overlays are superior to clear overlays (a placebo control) and to grey overlays that reduce the contrast and brightness (luminance) by a similar amount, (2) that quite different colours can be beneficial, although (3) the chosen colour appears to give the greatest benefit, (4) a complementary or aversive overlay colour gives relatively little benefit, but does not actually reduce reading speed, (5) the rate of reading is unaffected by motivational instructions.

Reliability and consistency

One of the most important aspects of any ability test is its reliability. A test is reliable if it gives the same result when administered more than once. Is the assessment of overlays reliable in this way? Further studies [13], attempted to answer this question. A year group of children in a middle school were examined. First the children were tested as a group and were asked about symptoms of distortion and discomfort when viewing text. All the children were then examined individually by different examiners using slightly different methods in two sessions no more than 3 days apart. One method resembled that described in Chapter 10 and the other method involved the initial comparison of each overlay with the white page. The same number of children, 78 (87%), chose a coloured overlay on both test sessions. The rate of reading with and without the overlay on Session 1 was strongly correlated with the rate of reading with and without the overlay on Session 2. An improvement in reading speed was measured by taking the reading speed with the overlay and dividing it by that without the overlay. Overall there was an 11% improvement in reading speed with the chosen overlay. The ratio obtained in Session 1 was strongly correlated with that obtained in Session 2, even though different overlays were sometimes chosen. Despite the differences in assessment method, 47% of children selected the same colour on both occasions and a further 21% chose an overlay of similar colour (neighbouring chromaticity). The consistency demonstrated by the children was very considerably above that expected on the basis of chance alone, but could, of course, have reflected memory for the colour previously chosen. Nevertheless, the children who chose exactly the same colour consistently on the two testing sessions showed a greater improvement in reading speed with that colour than those children who chose a similar colour. These children in turn showed a greater improvement in speed than those who chose a different colour on each test session, see Figure 8.1. Thus it would seem that children who derive a benefit from overlays find it easiest to chose those that are most beneficial.

In a further attempt to check that the specific colour chosen was critical [13] all the 378 children in a middle school in Norwich were examined individually with overlays. They were then given an overlay of a randomly chosen colour for a few months before being given the chosen overlay. The overlay was used longer among the children who, by chance, received an overlay of the colour they had chosen. The length of time the overlay was used decreased with the difference in chromaticity between

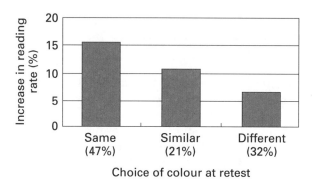

Figure 8.1. Percentage of increase in reading rate among children who chose the same colour at retest, a similar colour (neighbouring chromaticity), and a different colour, with the percentage of children in each category shown in parentheses.

its colour and the colour chosen. In other words, overlays that had a colour similar to that chosen were used longer than those with a different colour. This seems to confirm that the benefit is greatest with the chosen colour in a way that is independent of the tendency of children to conform.

Symptoms

The above studies demonstrate that the use of coloured overlays can improve reading rate, but what of visual stress? In one of the above studies [13] the children were asked questions while they looked at the text of the *Rate of Reading Test* (on this occasion printed in a 12pt sans serif font). They were asked: "Do the letters stay still or do they move?", "Are they clear or are they blurred (fuzzy, difficult to see)?", "Are the words too close together or far enough apart?", "Is the page too bright, not bright enough, or just about right?" and "Does it hurt your eyes to look at the page or is it OK?".

The symptoms reported during an initial testing of classes as a group were similar to those reported when the children were later examined individually. This suggests that the individual differences in the symptoms reported are consistent.

The 78 children who chose an overlay reported an average of 2.8 symptoms when questioned as a group, whereas the 11 who did not choose an overlay reported only 1.0 on average. Of children who showed an increase in reading rate of 30% or more, 83% reported four or more symptoms on the group test. Conversely, 63% of those who reported less than 4 symptoms showed an increase in reading rate of less than 30%.

Suppose we wished to identify the children whose reading speed would increase with an overlay by 30% or more. We could get a good idea simply on the basis of symptoms. If we identified the children reporting 4 or more symptoms, we would then have correctly identified 83% of the children who would show the required increase in speed. We would have missed 13%. We would have correctly rejected 63% of those who would not show an increase and unnecessarily tested 37%. This suggests that symptoms may be a useful indication of the likely benefit from filters, but they are not an infallible guide.

Reading strategy

Do the children who benefit from overlays differ from others in the strategies they use when reading? Some children sound words out when they read, others take in the whole word. In a preliminary study to address the issue we assessed children's strategy by looking at the way they spelled words. Phonologically regular words such as "steamer" can be read aloud correctly even if the word is unfamiliar, simply from a knowledge of the component shape-to-sound correspondence of the groups of letters (grapheme-phoneme conversion rules). Phonologically irregularly spelled words such as "yacht" on the other hand cannot be read correctly unless the word is familiar. Children aged 8–12 were asked to read a set of regular and irregularly spelled words. There was nothing to suggest that the children who used overlays differed from those who did not regarding the use of a phonological strategy [13].

Prevalence

In most of the studies reviewed so far we tested unselected children in mainstream education, usually testing entire classes, but sometimes entire schools. We wanted to avoid the difficulties of interpretation that can arise when children are selected for testing because their reading is poor, or because their reading is poorer than would be expected on the basis of their other skills. Nevertheless a surprisingly large proportion of the normal children we tested seemed to find overlays helpful. In order to estimate this proportion better, we needed a larger sample. In the next study all the children in Year 3 in 12 Norfolk schools were individually examined with the *Intuitive Overlays* [13]. Initially 60% of the 426 children reported a reduction of visual distortions, or improved comfort with one or more coloured overlays. These children were issued with an overlay of their chosen colour free of charge. In the summer term, about eight months later, 52% of these children (i.e. 31% of the total sample) were still using the overlay. The percentage of children using the overlay varied somewhat from one school to another (with a mean of 30% and standard deviation of 15 between schools). The prevalence is similar to that obtained in other studies [8, 14, 15, 28]. The children who were still using their overlays in the summer term were more likely to be those who in the previous autumn term read faster with their overlays than without them on the *Rate of Reading Test*. For whatever reasons, 5% of children read more than 25% faster with their overlay.

One might expect that a higher proportion of children who have been identified with reading problems would benefit from overlays. Surprisingly, in studies that have selected children with a diagnosis of dyslexia and a statement of special educational needs the proportion of children who benefit from overlays is similar to that in normal children [29]. Grounds and Wilkins (in preparation) compared four different groups: (1) children who had a diagnosis of dyslexia, (2) those without dyslexia but with similar chronological age, or (3) with similar reading age, or (4) with both similar chronological and reading age but with general intellectual impairment. There was no difference between the four groups with respect to the proportion who benefited from overlays. Thus a diagnosis of dyslexia does not seem to make it more likely that reading will benefit from coloured filters.

The prevalence of benefits in the adult population may be similar to those in children [30]. The number of people who can benefit from overlays is therefore very high.

Colour choice

In the large-scale study described above, the choice of colour was widely distributed among the colours available. The most frequently chosen colours, rose and aqua, were chosen by less than 10% of the sample of children. There was no particular difference in the frequencies with which the various colours were chosen by children who continued to use their overlays and those who ceased to use them. Thirty-three children chose the Grey overlay and, as mentioned above, these children did not show a reliable increase in reading rate with the overlay. Neither the children who chose the Grey overlay nor the children who were given one having chosen a different colour continued to use the Grey overlay. There was no relationship between the colour children regarded as their "favourite colour" and the colour they chose in an overlay.

In recent work we reported a relationship between the colour chosen and the child's ability to focus (accommodation) [28]. The children who chose overlays which reflected predominantly longer wavelengths (rose, orange, and yellow) tended to show greater accommodation. This is to be expected from the physics of refraction and is known to optometrists as the "duochrome effect". The relationship was, however, very weak.

Reading rate and reading skill

The children who used overlays had slightly poorer scores on standardised reading tests of the kind that schools use to assess a child's reading ability [13]. As might be expected, the good readers were generally the faster readers, as assessed by the *Rate of Reading Test*. Nevertheless, there were good readers (reading quotient more than 120) who read only 40 words per minute on the *Rate of Reading Test*. There were others with similar reading attainment who read more than *three times* as fast. These very large differences in reading speed among children with similar reading ability are curious, particularly because scores on the *Rate of Reading Test* are highly reliable from test to re-test [26]. It is possible that some of the differences are attributable to visual factors, rather than more general aspects of reading ability. Support for this position comes from the large number of individuals who report improved clarity with overlays, and also from the following observations concerning the design of text in children's reading books.

Design of children's text is not optimal

When children start to learn to read, their reading material has text that is at least twice the size and spacing of that read by adults. The text gets smaller and more closely spaced as the children learn, so that by the time they are 9 or 10 years of age the text has size and spacing similar to adult reading material. Does the text get smaller at a rate that is appropriate for the age and development of children? Recent evidence suggests not. It appears that the text gets too small much too quickly. Versions of the *Rate of Reading Test* were made with text size and layout that closely resembled the text in each of two popular reading schemes at four reading stages. In this way the effects of typeface and spacing could be examined independently of the linguistic difficulty of the material. The texts were all of similar reading difficulty, consisting simply of the same 15 common words in a different random order on each line; they differed only as regards type size and spacing, see Figure 8.2 which shows extracts. The reading speed of children aged 5 to 8 decreased as the text size decreased. The children aged 6–8 read the text designed for younger children more quickly than the text they were normally required to read. Older children aged 9 to 10 were neither assisted nor disadvantaged by text size over the range examined. Children of all ages, particularly those with visual stress, tended to make more errors on the smaller text rather than on the larger text. It looks very much as though the reading development of some children might benefit from a larger text size and spacing than is currently the norm, and that no children would be disadvantaged by such a change. It is possible that the benefit from overlays is partly attributable to the poor design of printed material for children. Publishers need to provide for teachers reading schemes in which the linguistic content becomes more complex *without* an associated decrease in type size and spacing.

What about the large-scale books that are used in the National Curriculum literacy strategy, which children have to read from a distance? Even though the print in these books appears large when viewed from close up, the text is too small and too closely spaced for viewing from the required distance [31]. In fact the text in some Big Books is too small to be seen, let alone read at the typical reading distances. The maximum reading distance should be 3 metres (half the current recommended maximum), and some readers may need to be even closer.

Reading silently for comprehension

The *Rate of Reading Test* uses meaningless material that the individual is required to read aloud. The reading involved therefore differs from normal reading which takes place silently and requires comprehension

(a)

cat for the yo
dog see to is

(b)

cat for the you n
is come play loc

(c)

cat for the you no
play look and see

(d)

cat for the you not
play look and see y
my the up and com

Figure 8.2. Extracts from the text used in the study by Hughes and Wilkins [31]. The text had size and spacing similar to that in popular reading schemes with extracts a–d being designed to be read by children aged 5–8 respectively.

of the material. It seemed important, therefore, to check that the reading speed measured by the *Rate of Reading Test* was pertinent to more normal reading. Ashby and Wilkins (unpublished data) therefore measured the improvement in reading speed with overlays on two tests. One test was the *Rate of Reading Test* and the other was a test that required silent reading with understanding. The latter test (The Speed and Capacity of Language Processing Task, otherwise known as the Baddeley Silly Sentences Test [32]), required children to read a series of simple sentences, such as "fruits grow on trees", "we eat shoes" and "fathers have wings for flying". They were required to classify the sentences as true or false and place a tick or cross beside each as appropriate. They were given two minutes in which to complete as many sentences as possible. Both tests were given to 29 children with reading difficulties, aged 8–16, who had been referred to the Norfolk Sensory Support Service. The tests were given with and without an overlay in random order. The overlay covered the textual material but left the right margin uncovered for the children to enter their responses. The rate of reading was clearly correlated with the rate at which the sentences were classified as true or false.[1] The percentage

[1] The correlation was statistically significant: $\rho = 0.69$, $p < 0.01$ without an overlay, and $\rho = 0.81$, $p < 0.01$ with.

improvement with an overlay on one test was found to be related to that on the other test.[2] These findings indicate that when the use of an overlay results in a large increase in performance on the *Rate of Reading Test*, an increase in speed is also to be expected in natural reading tasks.

Brightness of lighting

The lighting levels recommended for non-residential buildings have shown an increase over time between 1930–1970 followed by stabilisation or decline. The current recommendations for general lighting in schools show a 2–3 fold variation from one country to another but are on average close to the European recommendation. This recommended lighting level (300 lux) [33] is greater than that normally achieved in the home. Classrooms are usually brightly lit by daylight and artificial lighting and lighting levels are sometimes more than four times the recommended figure (author's observations). Reading in some classrooms is rather like reading in a glasshouse! Under these conditions children often find double overlays of use. In the studies of school children reviewed above, approximately half chose double overlays. They are much less likely to select double overlays in the modest lighting conditions of an optometry examination room. It is therefore important for an examination with overlays to be conducted under lighting conditions that resemble those in the individual's classroom or workplace. As we saw in Chapter 7, this is important not only because of the light level, but also because of the difference in colours that various types of lighting provide.

Conclusion

Scientific evidence clearly indicates that coloured overlays can improve reading speed and comfort in certain susceptible individuals. It is no longer reasonable to attribute the improvements to chance, suggestibility, motivation, or the influence of peers, teachers, or parents. Simple quick tests have been developed that make it easy to test whether colours can

---

[2] The correlation was statistically significant: $\rho = 0.55$, $p < 0.01$.

---

help a reader. At least 5% of the school population reads considerably faster with an overlay, with a further 20% benefiting to a lesser extent. A large proportion of the adult population may also benefit. Many issues remain unresolved, such as when, and whether benefits from coloured overlays indicate a likely benefit from coloured glasses.

nine

An illustrative case history: David's story

> A history based upon a report written by Elizabeth Ashby of the Norfolk Sensory Support Service

David was born in November 1980, the second of three children. He was four weeks premature, and was given 100% oxygen, but there was no evidence of any damage to the eyes. Most of his developmental milestones were normal although speech was slightly delayed, and he did not have a vocabulary of 20 words until aged two. Hand preference was unclear until age 4 when he established a preference for the left hand. David's mother suffered from migraines.

David began to read between the ages of 5–6 and initially progress was normal. His mother noticed that he always read more fluently when text below the line he was reading was covered. His mother retained his school reports. At age $5\frac{1}{2}$ he was noted to be "enjoying his reading" and there had been "an improvement in written work both in presentation and quantity". At age $7\frac{1}{2}$ he was making "steady progress" with reading, and his written work was "adequate". At age $9\frac{1}{2}$ the teacher commented "his reading has made steady progress ... he does not find spellings easy, but I feel David works to the best of his ability in all his written work". However problems became apparent by age $10\frac{1}{2}$. He was described as hard working but he tended "to take an inordinate time to complete any piece of work". Progress was considered "disappointing", and a note was made of "his reading difficulty" and the need "to work extremely hard if he is not to fall even further behind". At age 11 David's reading and spelling ages were two years behind his chronological age and he was assessed by Mona McNea, author of the Step-by-Step programme for students with dyslexia. She did not consider him to have specific learning difficulties, and did not detect problems with phonological awareness. He was assessed by a speech therapist who did not note any abnormality. He was also examined annually by an optometrist who found no significant refractive error and noted that stereopsis and colour vision were normal.

David was first assessed for Meares–Irlen syndrome by the Norfolk Sensory Support Service in June 1995 at the age of 15 when he was receiving extra support from the specific learning difficulties unit at his school. He described visual difficulty which affected him in all reading and writing activities. He complained that he could see the first two lines on the page clearly but that clarity deteriorated as he continued to read. The letters blurred, vibrated and jumbled, and he experienced frequent double vision. As a result he would abandon reading after only one page. His tracking was poor and he skipped or repeated lines. He could not copy from the board. His spelling and presentation were poor. He was unable to complete written assignments and was frequently reprimanded for lack of effort. He experienced frequent headaches and his eyes were constantly inflamed.

He selected a purple overlay as giving the most improvement. It was reported to prevent the blurring and movement of print, and reduce glare from the page. With the overlay he was able to read for sustained periods without experiencing fatigue and discomfort, and the frequency and severity of his headaches was reduced.

On 23 April 1996 David's reading speed on the *Rate of Reading Test* was 46 words per minute without the overlay and 103 with. When the text was printed widely spaced the reading speed without the overlay increased from 46 to 89 and with the overlay from 103 to 128 words per minute.

David was examined with the Intuitive Colorimeter in June 1996 and prescribed purple lenses. He found the lenses more beneficial and convenient than the overlay. Three months after he obtained the lenses his teachers confirmed an improvement in literacy skills, including presentation and quantity in English, science, and mathematics.

In September 1996 his reading was reassessed using the *Rate of Reading Test*. His reading speed without the overlay or lenses had increased to 99 words per minute. This suggests that the reduction of perceptual distortion with coloured filters had improved reading skills. A placebo control was introduced during this assessment. David was shown a grey overlay and told that this was a prototype offering an advancement in technology. He was told that he was one of the first to use it, and asked to do his best. With the grey overlay he then read 104 words per minute. With the purple overlay he read 125 words per minute. These results indicate that the motivational instructions had a very small effect compared with the effect of colour.

David is now 21 and has joined the Navy. He is still using the purple glasses. He reads books and is doing well in his studies. His confidence has increased and his mother is convinced that he would not be making the progress he is without his glasses.

ten

How to test whether overlays will be helpful

> ➤ Commercially available overlays
> ➤ Suggested test procedure
> ➤ A suitable reading task
> ➤ Double overlays
> ➤ Measuring effects on reading fluency

The following chapter provides a how-to-do-it guide for teachers, optometrists, and other professionals. It indicates how overlays are best selected, and how to evaluate their effectiveness.

There are several packs of overlays on the market. It is important to choose a pack that has a wide range of colours, and that permits one overlay to be placed on top of another to sample stronger colours. The *Intuitive Overlays* and the Cerium Overlays are suitable. Sheets of coloured plastic from stationers are not generally adequate because they do not provide a sufficiently wide range of subtle shades of colour.

The following procedure is based upon the *Intuitive Overlays*, supplied by iOO Sales. It can easily be adapted for use with the Cerium Overlays.[1] The test procedure is proposed because it is quick, simple, and efficient. The procedure elicits symptoms of visual-perceptual distortion, finds a colour that reduces these distortions, and measures any associated increase in reading fluency. The text on the Test Page (see Appendix 1) is

---

[1] The techniques described here were originally used by *Tintavision*, although this company has now evolved methods of its own. The methods currently used by this company have not been described in peer-reviewed scientific journals and no scientific evaluation of the methods has yet been published.

used: (1) to fatigue the eyes, (2) to elicit symptoms of perceptual distortion, (3) to compare the effects of different overlays, and (4) to compare the rate of reading with and without an overlay. It is important to select the text so that the size of the lettering is similar to that in text the individual is likely to be required to read. Several alternative texts have been printed in Appendix 1 and may be photocopied. Choose the text that has lettering of an appropriate size. The spacing of the letters has been deliberately compromised.

Suggested test procedure

You will need:

▪ A pack of overlays that samples many colours systematically.
▪ The Test Page. (If you are a testing a child, choose a text from Appendix 1 that has the size of lettering that the individual is currently being required to read. You can photocopy the page to suit your requirements.)
▪ The Record Sheet. (You can photocopy this from Appendix 2.)
▪ The Rate of Reading Score Sheet. (This can be photocopied from Appendix 3.)
▪ Room lighting that is typical of the workplace or classroom.
▪ A table at which you can sit beside the individual being tested without getting in the way of the light.
▪ A stopwatch to time the reading task, or, better still, a timer that can be set to ring after one minute has elapsed.
▪ A calculator to calculate the improvement in reading speed due to the overlay.
▪ A red and a blue pen to mark the Record Sheet.

Position the Test Page on the table in front of the person being tested at a comfortable reading distance (about 40 cm from the eyes).

Place the Grey overlay on the page with the gloss side uppermost and check that from where the person is sitting no light sources (room lights or windows) are reflected by the surface of the overlay. If they are, reposition the test materials.

Figure 10.1. Find a place where you can sit beside the person you are testing and where the lighting is typical of that person's classroom or workplace.

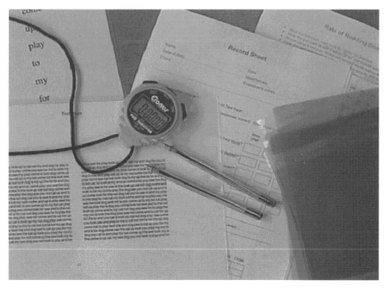

Figure 10.2. The materials needed for testing.

Familiarisation with the reading task

Will the person be able to read all the words on the Test Page? If in doubt, ask them to read the top line aloud. If the person cannot read the words, go straight to the questions on the Record Sheet and miss the next step.

Ask the person to read the passage out loud as quickly as possible (reading tires the eyes so that the symptoms are more likely):

▨ explain that the reading is for practice;
▨ explain that it will not make sense and will therefore sound strange;
▨ stop them after about 30 seconds;

While the person is still looking at the text, read the questions listed on the Record Sheet:

▨ Do the letters stay still or do they move?
▨ Are they clear or are they blurred (fuzzy, difficult to see)?
▨ Are the words too close together or far enough apart?
▨ Does it hurt your eyes to look at the page or is it OK?

Note the answers in the first column beside the questions. The greater the number of reported symptoms, the greater the chance that an overlay will be useful.

Finding the best overlay

Put the overlays in a pile in the following order from top to bottom;

1   Rose

2   Lime-green

3   Blue

4   Pink

5   Yellow

6   Aqua

7   Purple

8   Orange

9   Mint-green

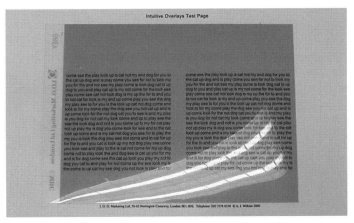

Figure 10.3. Check for glare from windows and lamps, and reposition the overlays if necessary.

Figure 10.4. Do the letters stay still or move?

Figure 10.5.   Place the top overlay over one side of the Test Page.

(The above colours are those used in the *Intuitive Overlays*, omitting Grey, which seldom helps: other packs have slightly different colours. The above sequence can be approximated with other packs. There is nothing magic about the sequence. Its purpose is simply to reduce the chances of similar or opposite (complementary) colours being placed next to each other.)

Take the top overlay and place it over the left-hand side of the Test Page, matt side uppermost. Ask the person which side (left or right) is clearest and most comfortable to see.

If the white side is clearest, remove the overlay and replace it with the next one from the pile.

If the coloured side is the better, turn the overlay over and check whether it is better with the matt side or gloss side uppermost. If the gloss side is better, use this side with the remaining overlays.

Leave the overlay in place with the best side uppermost. Take the next overlay from the pile and place it on the other side of the test page so that both sides are now covered by coloured overlays.

Again, ask the person which side is clearest and most comfortable to see.

Continue in this way. Each time leave the best colour in place and replace the poorer colour with the next overlay in the pile. Stop when you get to the bottom of the pile.

Figure 10.6. Check whether the overlay is better with the matt or gloss side uppermost.

If the person cannot make up their mind, make a note of both colours. Change one of the colours and continue. Re-introduce the other colour at the end of the pile.

Check that that final choice of overlay is better than no overlay. If it is, note the final choice of overlay (best single overlay) on the Record Sheet. If the white page is preferred to all the overlays, stop testing.

When you have selected the best overlay, cover one of the passages of text on the test page with the overlay and cover the other passage with white paper. Ask the person to look at the text covered by the chosen overlay. Ask the questions on the Record Sheet again. Note the answers in the second column. The greater the reduction in symptoms the more likely the overlay is to be beneficial.

Does the best single overlay colour reduce the distortions, but not get rid of them completely? If so, try stronger colours from double overlays as described in the following text.

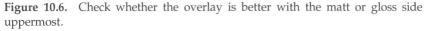

Are stronger colours better?

Stronger (more saturated) colours of similar hue can be obtained using two overlays placed one on top of another to create double overlays. Only

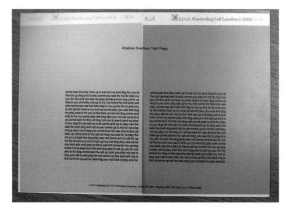

Figure 10.7. Leave the best overlay in place and place the next overlay beside it.

the combinations shown in the outer ring of Figure 7.1 are needed to sample colours systematically, as discussed in Chapter 7.

The pack of overlays should have two overlays of each colour. In the outer ring of Figure 7.1 find the three pairs of double overlays that border on the best single overlay. If the best single overlay was Rose, for example, these would be Rose Rose, Rose Orange, and Pink Rose. It does not matter which overlay is on top.

Arrange the best single overlay so that it covers both passages of text on the test page. Now make up one of the double overlays by placing an additional overlay over one side of the test page.

Ask the person whether the double overlay is better. Try each of the three double overlays in turn. If the stronger colours are better, find the best of the three.

For example, if the best single overlay was Rose, you would place a Rose overlay over both sides of the text. You would then take an additional Rose overlay and place it over one side only. You would ask which side was best. You would leave the best side as it is. On the other side you would show another of the double overlays. If the double Rose overlay was on the better side you would simply place a Pink overlay over the other side. If the single Rose overlay was on the best side, you would remove the additional rose overlay from the other side and replace it with the Pink overlay. You would then repeat this process with the additional Orange overlay.

Finally, position the double overlay over one of the passages of text and cover the other passage with white paper. Ask the questions on the Record Sheet a third time, and note the answers in the third column.

Measuring the effect of the colour on reading speed

These steps are necessary only if you wish to measure the effects of the overlays on reading speed in order to assess any benefit from the overlay, or to predict whether or not the overlay is likely to be used. Cover half the Test Page with a sheet of plain white paper so that only one passage can be seen. Tell the person you are going to ask them to read the text covered by the overlay(s). Then:

- Ask them to read aloud as quickly as possible, as before.
- Time them with a stopwatch.
- Use the Record Sheet to follow their reading. Using a red pen, strike out omitted words; ignore inserted words. If a line is missed out, put brackets at the beginning and end of the line. This is less obvious than crossing the line out.
- Stop the reading after a minute.
- Mark the text thus // on the Record Sheet to show where the person got to.
- Note the total number of words correctly read. A word must be in the right place to be correct, so omitted words and lines must be subtracted. If a pair of words is reversed in order, only one of the pair counts.

Remove the overlay(s). Ask the person to read the passage on the white page, again for a minute, noting the errors as before, using a blue pen.

Calculate the percentage increase in reading speed with the overlay as follows:

- take the number of words read with the coloured overlay;
- divide it by the number of words read with no overlay;
- take the result and subtract 1;
- take this result and multiply by 100.

If the percentage increase is greater than 5, the overlay is likely to be of use. Issue the overlay from a dispensing pack. Don't give your testing overlays away!

Figure 10.8. Double overlays are examined by placing an overlay over both passages of text and other overlays over one or both sides.

Figure 10.9. To measure reading speed, cover one of the passages on the Test Page with paper. Compare the reading speed of the other passage when it is covered by an overlay and when it is uncovered.

Rate of Reading Score Sheet

- Hear the passage read once for 30 seconds as practice.
- Hear the passage of text read aloud for one minute with overlay.
- Score using a red pen. Strike out omitted words below. Mark finish thus //.
- Hear the passage read aloud again for one minute, this time without the overlay.
- Score using a blue pen. Strike out omitted words below. Mark finish thus //.

come 1	see 2	the 3	play 4	look 5	up 6	is 7	cat 8	not 9	my 10	and 11	dog 12	for 13	you 14	to 15
the 16	cat 17	up 18	dog 19	and 20	is 21	play 22	come 23	you 24	see 25	for 26	not 27	to 28	look 29	my 30
you 31	for 32	the 33	and 34	not 35	see 36	my 37	play 38	come 39	is 40	look 41	dog 42	cat 43	to 44	up 45
dog 46	to 47	you 48	and 49	play 50	cat 51	up 52	is 53	my 54	not 55	come 56	for 57	the 58	look 59	see 60
play 61	come 62	see 63	cat 64	not 65	look 66	dog 67	is 68	my 69	up 70	the 71	for 72	to 73	and 74	you 75
to 76	not 77	cat 78	for 79	look 80	is 81	my 82	and 83	up 84	come 85	play 86	you 87	see 88	the 89	dog 90
my 91	play 92	see 93	to 94	for 95	you 96	is 97	the 98	look 99	up 100	cat 101	not 102	dog 103	come 104	and 105
look 106	to 107	for 108	my 109	come 110	play 111	the 112	dog 113	see 114	you 115	not 116	cat 117	up 118	and 119	is 120
up 121	come 122	look 123	for 124	the 125	not 126	dog 127	cat 128	you 129	to 130	see 131	is 132	and 133	my 134	play 135
is 136	you 137	dog 138	for 139	not 140	cat 141	my 142	look 143	come 144	and 145	up 146	to 147	play 148	see 149	the 150

Figure 10.10. The Score Sheet in Appendix 3 shows the number of words read underneath each word. Mark omitted words by crossing them out, mark transpositions by a curved line as shown, and mark omitted lines with brackets at each end. Mark the end of the minute with //. If you use different pen colours you can use the same score sheet to mark the reading performance achieved with and without the overlay.

Note. Although the effects of practice on the rate of reading are small, there is nevertheless some variability, and in borderline cases it can be useful to give the test more than once. Give the test with the overlay, without it, again without it and then again with it. Average the scores with, and without the overlay.

The advantage of measuring the effect of an overlay on reading rate is that it provides a measure of the extent to which the overlays improve reading, and it helps to predict whether the overlays will be useful in the long term. If the increase in reading speed is greater than 5% the overlays are likely to be used for more than three months.

65

My son has been prescribed tinted lenses to help with his reading. He is just eleven years old and found that the words jumped when he read. He received his new glasses at the beginning of March. Last week he had another reading test. The test last November gave him a reading age of 10 years 9 months. Last week with his tinted glasses, his reading age has gone up to 13 years 3 months.

Parent

Reading speed improved from 42 words per minute to 130 with lens! School delighted. Sophie's confidence increased, now enjoys lessons – no longer receiving special needs teaching – SATs results excellent.

Parent of 10-year-old girl

Kelly has had the tinted lenses for one year and her reading age has gone from 8 years to 11 years. I put this down to the tinted lenses. We noticed a difference within a month.

Parent of 14-year-old girl

Andrew says his glasses are of great benefit to him. The words no longer jump around. He finds it difficult to read without them. Andrew's school report noted he was happy to read aloud in class and read with confidence, something he would never have done before.

Parent of 12-year-old boy

Jack, now aged 9, has been wearing his green glasses for nearly $2\frac{1}{2}$ years. He continues to wear them for maths and reading. He says it takes the 'sting' out of the white paper and helps him to concentrate. He wears them voluntarily, with no prompting at all.

Parent

eleven

Who to test using overlays: a guide for teachers

> ➤ How to identify individuals who might benefit on the basis of their symptoms

> ➤ A cost-effective screening

There is no hard and fast rule for predicting whether someone will find an overlay helpful. The only certain way of finding out is to test with overlays and give the chosen overlay to the person to use for a trial period. Ideally every pupil should be examined in this way because about 1 in 5 children in mainstream education experience some benefit from overlays. One in 20 derive considerable benefit, reading more than 25% faster with their overlay. Some of these have no symptoms and are not obviously underachieving in reading.

It will not usually be practical to examine all pupils individually, and so it is important to identify those who are most likely to benefit and concentrate on them.

Firstly, pupils who benefit from overlays are more likely to be the children whose reading is poorer than you would expect, given their other skills. If you have children who concern you in this way, begin with them. Secondly, pupils who experience perceptual distortions of text are more likely to benefit from overlays. You will not usually be aware of the distortions unless you question the pupil, and even then children may consider the distortions normal or be too embarrassed to complain. They may not even be aware of the distortions until the distortions are removed by a coloured overlay.

Nevertheless, by asking children questions about what they see when they look at text, it is possible to increase the chances of identifying the children who are most likely to benefit from an overlay.

Figure 11.1. Group testing.

Children's reports of distortions are most reliable if the questions are asked in the here-and-now. The children should be looking at the text when you ask them what they see and feel. The distortions may take time to appear, so children may need to have been exposed to print for a while before testing. The five questions listed in the Record Sheet (Appendix 2) and the Group Test Sheet (Appendix 4) have been found to be among the best. You may need to explain to young children what "blurred" means (fuzzy, hard to see).

All of the children whose reading speed increases considerably (more than 30%) with an overlay may be expected to report at least two of these symptoms. More than 80% should report at least four.

If you were to test all the children who report two or more symptoms, you could expect most to show an increase in reading speed. In 70% of those with two or more symptoms the increase in speed should be at least 10%.

---

1 A suggestion

Teachers might consider examining the symptoms of all the children in their class as a group. Here are the steps to take:

- Photocopy the Group Test Sheet in Appendix 4 and give a copy to each child in the class. Ask children to enter their first names and family names, class, and date.
- Check to make sure all children who use/need glasses for reading are wearing them.
- Explain that the text on the sheet may look difficult but it uses only words that are easy to read, and list these on the board. Explain that the text does not mean anything.
- Ask the children to read the text aloud for a minute. You could say to them, "In the middle of the page you can see a block of writing. Each line has those same 15 words. They are the easy words we read on the board. I want you to read them out loud as fast as you can. Each of you is going to read the words as fast as you can, without waiting for each other. I'm only going to give you a minute, so you won't get to the bottom, nobody does. You've got to keep going as quickly as you can. I want you to read it properly. I'll tell you when to start. Ready, steady, go . . .". Treat this as a game. The clamour that results is not as bad as you might expect!
- Ask them to continue looking at the text, while you read the questions given on the Group Test Sheet one at a time. Ask the children to put a tick in the appropriate box. For example, you might say, "Now I am going to ask you some questions about how the writing looks to you. There are no right or wrong answers. Only one person knows what you can see. Who's that person? You. Only you know the answers. But it is very important that you don't tell anybody else what you can see. You keep your answers completely to yourself. Every time I ask you a question I want you to look back at the writing and think about how to answer the question. First of all I want you to look at the writing and think about this question. Do the letters stay still or do they move? If you think they stay still, I want you to put a tick in the first box, but if you think they move put a tick in the second box. Then look back up, so I know you are ready . . .", and so on for the remaining questions.
- Begin your overlay screening by examining those children who report the most symptoms, and continue with the remaining children as time permits.

The rationale for the above test procedure is as follows:

- Reading the text aloud engages the class and helps ensure that each child looks at the print and tries to read it. In those susceptible to visual stress, the reading tires the eyes and makes the symptoms of stress appear.
- Asking the questions about symptoms of perceptual distortion provides a scale: the more symptoms reported, the worse the stress.
- Individuals who report more distortions are more likely to benefit from an overlay. You can begin by testing these children, and then test the remainder as time permits.
- The procedure is fun for the children to do, and it takes the class only 10–15 minutes.

twelve

Overlays and classroom management

Techniques for classroom management.

➤ Reading
➤ Writing
➤ Examinations
➤ Board work
➤ Lighting

This chapter lays down guidelines for classroom teachers.

1 Reading

Overlays should be used for tasks that require reading, not simply for "reading lessons". Discuss with the child which tasks are involved, and which lessons the overlay should be used for. It may be necessary to remind children to use them, but it is not advisable to insist a child uses an overlay if it is no longer helpful. A different colour may then be required, or it may be that the child no longer needs the overlay.

The overlay should not be creased, and it is a good idea to keep it in an envelope or plastic wallet when it is not in use. Pupils should feel able to use their finger as a marker when reading. Check the condition of the overlay every few weeks, and keep some spares! An extra overlay for use at home may be a good idea. The best colour under the lighting at home

· may differ from that at school, so you can ask parents to borrow a set of overlays to check at home.

It will be difficult, if not impossible for a child to share books while using an overlay. Not only is the overlay likely to interfere with a partner's reading, the individual who suffers visual stress needs to be able to orient the book to make the text easy to see. Some other provision needs to be made if there is a shortage of books.

If the distortions and discomfort persist despite an overlay, make a mask that covers lines above and below those being read to reveal 2 or 3 lines only.

If an overlay is used persistently for more than a school term, encourage the parents to obtain coloured glasses making them aware of the cost. These may make copying from the board easier.

2 Writing

It is a good idea to provide buff recycled paper for written tasks. This paper does not have whiteners. (Whiteners are substances, similar to those in washing powder, that convert ultraviolet light to visible light, making the paper literally "whiter than white"). It is a better idea, however, to allow the child to choose the colour of the paper from a large range of alternative colours. The best colour of paper will normally be similar to that of the best overlay. There are several suppliers of coloured paper, see links at www.essex.ac.uk/psychology/overlays.

Encourage pupils to experiment with differently coloured pens to find the colour that is easiest for them to read.

If pupils are allowed to write on every other line, the extra space will enable them to see what they have written more clearly. The extra space needs to be introduced both horizontally across the line as well as vertically between lines.

Pupils may need extra time to complete tasks. It is advisable to ensure that instructions are understood and notes are copied correctly and completely.

3 Examinations

Examination questions are sometimes printed on coloured paper to aid with sorting. It is then necessary for the questions to be photocopied onto white paper (so that the overlay gives the right colour). This may be better than photocopying the exam papers onto paper with the same colour as the overlay because it is often difficult to find exactly the right shade, and you will not have to make different copies for different children.

Candidates may need reminding to bring their overlays or glasses to the exam. Have spares available.

It may be helpful for candidates to present their written work on coloured paper with extra spacing of lines. Allow the candidate to choose the colour.

Candidates may now use coloured overlays or coloured papers without seeking prior permission from the awarding body, according to the Joint Council for General Qualifications' *Regulations and Guidance Relating to Candidates with Particular Requirements* [34].

4 Board work

Blackboards are usually less stressful to read from than white boards. You can ask the child to find out through experimentation which colours of pens/chalks are best for board work and for marking work. Pupils can then be made responsible for giving the appropriate pens to their teachers. Remember there may be pupils who require different colours!

Read the material aloud as it is written on the board. Use large lettering and check it can be seen. It may be difficult for a child to copy from the board, so personal copies should be provided if possible. A child should not be expected to copy from a neighbour, especially in lesson time. If possible, give extra time for copying.

5 Computers

The issues are complex and are covered in the next chapter.

6 Lighting

The child with Meares–Irlen syndrome should sit in natural lighting away from fluorescent lights if possible. Fluorescent lights usually flicker continuously 100 times per second.[1] Although the flicker cannot be seen, it affects eye movements adversely and can give headaches [2] – to which those with Meares–Irlen syndrome are particularly susceptible.

Curtains or blinds may be helpful in bright sunlight, although Venetian blinds can create an aversive striped pattern. Avoid standing in front of a Venetian blind when addressing the class. In general, classroom lighting levels are higher than they need to be. Your children may read more easily without the room lights on!

Coloured desk lights are available, but they are expensive and impractical in the classroom.

7 General

Deal with embarrassment, peer pressure and bullying.

Even if pupils clearly benefit from overlays or tinted lenses they may need reminding to use them. The required tint can change, however, so if the overlays or lenses are no longer helpful ensure the child has a further assessment. If a child is not using an overlay, try and find out what the reasons are, but remember that the child is the best judge of the effectiveness of an overlay.

Ensure all staff know that coloured glasses are prescribed for visual difficulties. Children should have a note to carry to inform supply staff.

Children with Meares–Irlen syndrome will tire quickly, even if they are using overlays or lenses and will benefit from short but frequent breaks.

With young children it is often difficult to know whether or not they benefit from an overlay, and which colour is the best. You can assess them over a long period, using different colours from day to day or week to week.

Above all, talk to the children about their difficulties and monitor the use of overlays and lenses.

If your school colleagues are reluctant to take the above issues seriously you can gently remind them that the disability sections of the Special Educational Needs and Disability Act 2001 is designed to ensure that children and young people with a disability are not discriminated against in education. The legislation says that a school discriminates against a disabled child if, for a reason related to the child's disability, it treats

[1] They flicker 120 times a second in countries with a 60-Hz electricity supply, such as the United States.

the child less favourably than others, and it cannot show that the treatment is justified. The school is required to anticipate the needs of disabled children and make reasonable adjustments to ensure that disabled pupils are not put at a substantial disadvantage [35].

Further ideas for classroom management can be found in a book by Rhonda Stone [36, pp. 171–178].

thirteen

Use of computers

> Variation from one machine to another
> Effects of refresh rate
> Characteristics of various operating systems
> Web software
> The importance of surround lighting
> Strategies for colour search
> Liquid crystal displays
> Text layout

Computers are a part of everyday life for many of us, including those of us who have dyslexia. Unfortunately many individuals suffer visual stress when they use computers. In this chapter we consider how such stress can be reduced.

Computers vary considerably. The operating systems vary, the application software varies, the displays vary, and the viewing conditions vary. All sources of variation are potentially of importance when it comes to reducing stress, and determining the background and foreground colours optimal for reading. (The foreground colours are those used for text or graphics.)

Most computer displays use a cathode ray tube similar to that in a television receiver. The picture is generated by a spot of light that zig-zags down the screen varying in brightness and colour as it goes. The spot "paints" the image and moves too quickly for the brain to perceive the motion. On most modern displays it takes less than one seventieth of a second for the screen to be "refreshed" from top to bottom (the refresh rate is greater than 70 Hz.[1] If you are aware of flicker, your screen may be operating at a refresh rate less than 70 Hz. Visible flicker is very tiring. Check to see whether your screen can be operated at a higher refresh rate. On machines with Windows 97 and above use the Control Panel to select Display Properties and then select the Settings tab.

On machines with Windows 3.1 and Windows 95 operating systems it is possible to change the background and foreground colours in any application by downloading a program written by Simon Hamer. The program, called *Tinter*, is available free of charge from http//:www. essex.ac.uk/psychology/overlays. The program brings up a window on the desktop with three sliders, one for brightness, one for hue and one for saturation. Buttons determine whether these sliders apply to the background or the foreground. *Tinter* can be run together with any other application. This means that it is possible for the user to be running their typical application (word processor, spreadsheet, etc.) while they adjust the background and foreground colours in the application's window.

Unfortunately, *Tinter* does not work in Windows 98 or later Windows operating systems. These operating systems allow some control over background and foreground colours but it is not possible to adjust the colours and immediately see the effect of the adjustment.

In addition to the options provided by the operating system, there are many applications, such as word processors, web browsers and spreadsheets that permit the background and foreground colours to be reset according to the user's preference. Only in rare cases is it possible to assess the effects of any change immediately without interfering with the window in which the application is running.

Depending on the brightness of the display relative to the brightness of the surroundings, the screen can appear to be either a source of coloured light or a coloured surface illuminated by ambient light. The colour optimal for surfaces and for light sources may differ because of adaptation. It will be pointed out in Chapter 16 that the colour optimal for use in overlays, a coloured surface, is not the same as that optimal in lenses which resemble a coloured light source. Although the basis for the difference is not entirely clear, colour adaptation is likely to be an important part of the

---

[1] When computers were first introduced, there were more complaints than there are now. This is partly because people have got used to computers, but also because the displays have improved. Flicker is more apparent when a lower refresh rate is used, and when computers were first introduced refresh rates of 60 Hz were typical. In European computers the refresh rate was sometimes even lower.

explanation. A computer display is usually self-luminous, but can be brighter or dimmer than the surroundings. These considerations suggest that the settings of a computer monitor should be selected by the user on their own computer in the lighting conditions in which they typically work. Settings obtained on a different computer in a different environment may not be optimal.

It is recommended that users begin by selecting the colour of background that is most comfortable. Choose weakly saturated colours to begin with until you find one that is comfortable. Then try more saturated versions of this colour. For example, in Word 97 you would go to the Format menu and select Background. Then click on More Colours and then Standard and select one of the colours close to white. Alternatively you can try selecting the colours from the system menus. In Windows 98 and 2000, for example, go to the Start menu, select Settings, choose Control Panel, then Display, then Appearance. Click on Window text and change the background colour. You will find that this colour appears in some system windows but not the windows of all applications.

If you are purchasing a new computer system and have the money, it is worth considering obtaining a liquid crystal thin film transistor (TFT) display. These screens now have a good spatial resolution and a good range of colours. Most important, however, the image is not created by a flying spot, and they do not flicker, even at high frequencies. Cathode ray tube displays always flicker. Even though the flicker frequency may be too high for you to be aware of, it can nevertheless interfere with the control of eye movements, and this can be tiring [2]. The interference with eye movements may be one reason why it is usually more effective to proof read text on paper than on screen.

So far we have considered only the colour of computer displays. But the size and spacing of text is at least as important as the colour. Choose a font that is as large as possible given the amount of text you need to see on the page at any one time. Choose a line spacing that is sufficiently large. Experiment with character spacing: some fonts are much clearer when the character spacing is increased by a fraction of a font-size.

Conclusion

No device in the history of written language has ever offered the flexibility provided by the computer. This flexibility could allow for the differences that exist in the way people see, but at present the software tools are insufficient for this task.

Having dyslexia and struggling with it over 27 years, the transformation and difference that my tinted lenses have made is unbelievable. I see text as "normal people" do, still and not moving around; all letters one shape or size. Following columns is easy – paragraphs stand alone instead of all flowing into one. I no longer take a deep breath at the thought of reading a letter, leaflet, or book. It has taken me a little while to adjust to the lenses, especially the colour. (I make) sure the light is on when doing office work, due to my glasses making my environment a little dark. Reading off colour sheets of paper can sometimes be a little difficult too. However I am delighted with the change my glasses have made to my life. I only wish they were on offer when I was younger. I hope that the young children of today . . . will be able to access and benefit . . . .

27-year-old woman

The glasses have given me a new lease of life. I can now read books without getting head and eye pain. As a dyslexic person I am now planning to go back to university and do a Diploma in Social Work, I never had the confidence to do this due to my reading problems. I still have a long battle ahead, but I remain positive.

41-year-old man

My son Adam is an 11-year-old dyslexic. He has been wearing precision tinted spectacles for 18 months. He started off by using a coloured plastic overlay to see if it made any difference to his reading. In the first twelve months his reading age improved from being 6 years 9 months to 8 years 10 months. This year he did the S.A.T.S. tests and almost gained level 4 by being 8 marks short of the national average in the test results. I feel that these spectacles have made a huge difference to Adam, and given him a lot of confidence.

Parent

Wearing tints has totally changed Dale's life. He no longer has headaches or feels sick after a lot of reading. His English grade at school went up two grades in a term and all of his schoolwork has improved very significantly. Listening to Dale read is like listening to a different child and his handwriting has improved. The best result of all of this is that Dale's confidence has doubled in the short time he has been using overlays and had his tints. If the government doesn't think this exists they should come and talk to the parents and teachers of the children involved and they would see what a difference tints make to their lives.

Parent of 11-year-old boy

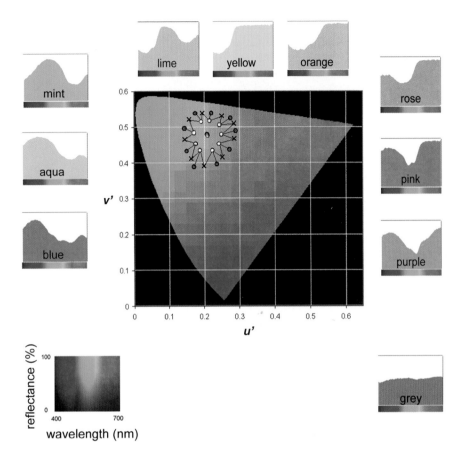

Plate 1. (Centre) Uniform Chromaticity Scale diagram of the International Lighting Commission [23] showing the chromaticities of the nine colour *Intuitive Overlays* (inner ring of white points) and grey overlay (central point). The chromaticities are those of the overlay when it is in contact with a white (spectrally uniform) page. The chromaticities of double overlays formed by placing one overlay on top of another are shown by the outer ring of points. The grey points are the chromaticities of two overlays of identical colour. The crosses mark the chromaticities of two overlays of neighbouring colours. The lines connect the chromaticities of the double overlays with those of constituent single overlays. (Periphery) Graphs showing the reflectance as a function of wavelength for each of the overlays, using the axes of the graph of the spectrum (lower left), are disposed around the perimeter as per their chromaticity, with the exception of grey. Note that the reflectance functions and chromaticities shown are for the overlays themselves and take no account of the illumination.

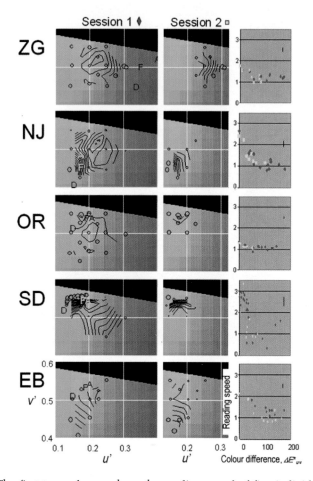

Plate 2. The first two columns show the reading speed of five individuals (rows) under light of different colours. The position of each point shows the chromaticity of the light, and the diameter of the point is directly proportional to the reading speed. Contours have been fitted using a computer algorithm (triangulation). The contours are similar in Session 2 despite the fewer data. The data have been replotted in the third column in terms of the difference in colour between the optimal colour and the colour under which the reading speed was measured. The reading speed is shown as a factor of the reading speed under white light ("1" shows reading speeds identical to that under white light, "2" shows reading speeds that are twice as fast, etc.). The steepness of the scatter of points shows the rate at which the reading speed declines with the difference in colour from the optimal. The vertical bars in each graph show the standard deviation of reading speed at each colour. The graphs show that a colour difference of 100 (equivalent to about eight just-noticeable differences) is sufficient to eliminate any advantage conveyed by colour. The chromaticity of a spectrally uniform surface viewed through the lenses and illuminated by incandescent light (CIE Type A), fluorescent light (CIE Type F3) or daylight (CIE Type D65), are shown in the first column by the letters A, F and D respectively.

fourteen

Meares–Irlen syndrome, dyslexia, and attention deficit/hyperactivity disorder

> ➤ The similarities and differences between Meares–Irlen syndrome, dyslexia, and attention deficit disorder are discussed.

Dyslexia is the most common of the specific learning difficulties and usually involves spelling as well as reading. There is no single definition of dyslexia that is universally accepted. Historically the term has been taken to refer to a difficulty with learning to read that cannot be explained in terms of a general intellectual deficit; a specific learning difficulty in which reading and/or spelling is markedly poorer than·that expected on the basis of age and intelligence. Sometimes this definition is made more specific to refer to individuals whose reading age is more than 2 years behind their chronological age. Although this is an objective definition that has been used in the past, it has the drawback that two years is arbitrary and refers to a level of deficit that varies with age. The Division of Educational and Child Psychology of the British Psychological Society has now moved away from the idea of dyslexia as a discrepancy between reading and other skills. In a recent report [37] it is argued that "dyslexia is evident when accurate and fluent word reading and/or spelling develops very incompletely or with great difficulty".

Given that Meares–Irlen syndrome interferes with reading, can it cause dyslexia? It depends on your definitions. Sometimes individuals who are recognised as dyslexic benefit greatly from coloured filters, but there are others who do not. Reading is a complex skill and one might expect reading failure and therefore dyslexia to have a multitude of possible mechanisms. Earlier in this book, I have drawn attention to the large proportion of the school population who read more quickly with coloured filters. Suppose we select only individuals with dyslexia defined in terms of a discrepancy between reading age and chronological age. Is the proportion who benefit in this population greater than in the population at large? Chapter 8 provided evidence that the answer to this question seems to be "only slightly if at all". A recent study (Grounds and Wilkins, in preparation) compared four groups: dyslexic individuals, individuals of similar age and normal reading ability, younger individuals with reading ability similar to that of the dyslexic individuals, and individuals whose reading was similar to that of the dyslexics because of a general intellectual difficulty. The four groups did not differ significantly with respect to the proportion of individuals who reported benefits from overlays and the number who read more quickly with them. Similar results have been reported by Kriss [29].

There are many subtle visual deficits in dyslexia that may occasionally occur in individuals with Meares–Irlen syndrome. For a review, see Evans [38]. One might anticipate that in Meares–Irlen syndrome, but not in dyslexia, the reading difficulty caused by perceptual distortion is likely to manifest itself as the text the child is required to read gets smaller and more closely spaced. Initially reading acquisition may progress quite normally until small closely spaced text is encountered. The child may then become reluctant to read because of discomfort and headaches.

In her book *The Light Barrier* [36, pp. 134–136], Rhonda Stone draws up a "chart of common traits" that helps to highlight the ways in which Meares–Irlen syndrome, dyslexia, and attention deficit/hyperactivity disorder (ADD/ADHD) resemble one another, and the ways in which they differ. The following can occur in *all three* disorders: skipping of words or whole lines during reading; loss of place when reading; slow reading; poor comprehension; aversion to reading; unequal letter size and spacing when writing; difficulty writing on the line; poor handwriting; restlessness or daydreaming; struggling to complete work; headaches, stomach aches, and fatigue; depression, frustration, or anger; poor self esteem; anxiety; difficulty making friends.

The following can occur in both Meares–Irlen syndrome and dyslexia: visual distortions of the printed page; experiencing reversals of letters; reading words that are upside down; mixing up numbers in maths problems.

The following are most common in Meares–Irlen syndrome: eyes burning itching or watering; frequent rubbing of the eyes; shading eyes when reading; screwing the eyes up or blinking excessively; tilting head to read; fatiguing after less than 15 minutes reading; reading in a dim light; seeing print as fuzzy or unstable; family history of strain with reading, light sensitivity, headaches, or migraine.

It is mainly those with dyslexia who are slow to learn to speak, who are slow to learn the connections between individual letters and sounds, who have difficulty sounding out words, who jumble up syllables in spoken and written words, who have difficulty telling the time, and who have difficulty following verbal directions. Verbal directions can also be a problem for individuals with ADD/ADHD but here this is associated with restlessness and lack of self-restraint.

As will be evident from the above, Meares–Irlen syndrome, dyslexia, and ADD/ADHD can share certain symptoms. This does not necessarily mean that the symptoms have the same cause, or can be treated in the same way. Nevertheless, it makes sense to reduce visual stress and distortions where present, and coloured filters are one way of doing so in some individuals.

I first discovered that tinted lenses could help me about 3–4 years ago. I had always struggled with reading and at school and college I read the bare minimum that I could get away with. My eyes would tire and I found it difficult to focus as the words seemed to hover over the page instead of being on the paper, giving a 3D effect. I did not realise this was happening until I saw the difference with the tint. To help focus I would lay a piece of paper under the line I was reading to cover up the other text which interfered with my focus as it was all moving on the page, similar to the movement when reading in a car. Reading made me feel sick, like carsickness. My first pair of tinted glasses was chosen using coloured acetate sheets placed over a page of text. My new lenses were chosen using the machine. The yellow colour I chose is much darker and even better than before. I feel I got a more exact match for my eyes this time. I find it difficult to put into words how tinted lenses have changed my life. I am able to read an entire newspaper without stopping and I even enjoy reading books. For people like myself you don't know you have a problem until you see the difference. You spend your life feeling inadequate, others think you are lazy, when the truth is that you work harder than anyone else to achieve the same.

35-year-old woman

I have had the glasses now for just over a year, and from the first day I put them on it's as if someone came along and turned the glare button down, like you would to the contrast dial on a TV. I can now do things that I avoided. I read more and they really help when I am out and about because reading street signs is now a doddle. The black writing doesn't run around a page of white paper anymore either . . . .

27-year-old man

They help me with reading and writing activities. They stop me from suffering with discomfort and migraines. Also I find them useful when watching TV etc.

16-year-old girl

fifteen

Coloured glasses

> ➤ History of tinted lenses
> ➤ When are coloured lenses preferable to overlays?
> ➤ The importance of colour precision
> ➤ Alternative systems for ophthalmic tints compared
> ➤ Differences between colours used in overlays and lenses
> ➤ Some common concerns discussed
> ➤ Technical details of the *Intuitive Colorimeter*, the colorimeter assessment and the design of coloured trial lenses

1   A little history

Coloured spectacle lenses are not recent: they have been with us for several centuries. The museum at the British College of Optometry has several pairs of spectacles with blue and green lenses dating from about 1800. The development in the use of coloured lenses has occurred only recently because it is only in the past few decades that it has become possible to dye lenses any colour to suit an individual. At first the technique was used for cosmetic tints, but gradually it is coming to be realised that the technical ability to provide any colour on an individual basis offers a new form of treatment for a wide variety of neurological disorders of the human visual system.

2 When are coloured glasses necessary?

If an individual clearly benefits from an overlay, it is worth considering coloured glasses as an alternative. Coloured glasses can be used for reading at a distance (e.g. reading the board in the classroom) and for reducing glare in situations other than reading, such as when writing. The colour of glasses can be selected with greater precision than with overlays, which may be one reason why the benefit from glasses is usually greater. They are more convenient than overlays, and more durable. It is not sufficient to select glasses from a range of cosmetic tints because the colour is insufficiently precise. A variety of systems have been developed to allow an individual to find the colour appropriate for their needs.

3 The importance of precision

In order to assess just how precise a tint needs to be for optimal effect, Dr Nirmal Sihra and I asked patients who wore coloured glasses to read passages of text illuminated by coloured light in the *Intuitive Colorimeter*. Two females and three males aged 11–17 took part.[1] We varied the colour of light (keeping brightness constant) so as to study the effect of colour on reading speed. The passages were of randomly ordered common words, each passage having a different order. The passages and the colours of the illumination were presented in a random order. The colour of the light changed randomly from one trial to the next. It was difficult for participants to keep track of what colours they had seen, and how the colour had affected their reading speed. It is therefore unlikely that their performance was affected by any expectations they might have had. Each row in Plate 2 presents the data for one patient. The first figure in each row shows data from the first session, the second shows data from the second session and the third figure is a graph. The positions of the points in each figure show the chromaticities of the light and the diameter of the points is proportional to the reading speed, larger points for faster reading. A computer

---

[1] All had been prescribed coloured glasses for the reduction of symptoms of visual stress when reading. None had uncorrected refractive error, untreated vergence insufficiency, or anomalous colour vision on clinical testing. All had continued using the glasses for 5 months to 3 years (average 18 months) prior to testing.

---

algorithm (triangulation) has been used to draw contours. The contours are similar to those that represent the hills on a geographic map. Contours on such a map connect the places of similar height and they are more closely spaced where a hill slopes more steeply. In this case the contours show colours where the reading speed is similar. Notice that in every case the contours obtained in Session 1 (first column) are very similar to those obtained in Session 2 (second column), indicating just how consistent is the variation of reading speed with colour. Each contour differs from its neighbour by 10% of the speed under white light. You can see that the reading speed can change very markedly as colour is changed only slightly. This is represented most dramatically in the graph in the third column, which shows how reading speed decreases as the colour differs from the optimum. The difference is expressed on the horizontal axis as CIE *LUV* colour difference [23], which is proportional to the distance between the two colours (chromaticities) on the UCS diagram (see Representing colours on a "map", in Chapter 6). Two neighbouring coloured surfaces can just be discriminated as different in colour when the colour difference between them is about 13 units.[2] The scatter of points in the graph shows that a difference of twice this value is sufficient to reduce the reading speed considerably. Reading speed is shown on the vertical axis of the graph in terms of the ratio of the reading speed under white light. A value of two indicates a reading speed twice that under white light. The graphs show that a colour difference of 100 is sufficient to reduce reading speed to that under white light.

Given that small differences in colour can be sufficient to change reading speed substantially, what of the variation in colour that occurs with changes in lighting? The colour provided by prescribed coloured spectacles varies with lighting conditions. In Plate 2 the letter A shows the chromaticity provided by the patient's spectacles under the light from a filament lamp (CIE illuminant A). The letter F shows the colour provided under the light from a "white" fluorescent lamp (CIE illuminant F3), and the letter D shows the colour provided by daylight (CIE illuminant D65). In general the chromaticities are close to those at which reading speed is optimal, with the instructive exception of the patient whose data are shown in the last row. This boy had been prescribed green glasses, as can be seen from the positions of the letters A, F, and D, but over the intervening year his symptoms had gradually returned. The contours show that his reading speed was now optimal under blue light. His tint prescription was revised and the symptoms abated. His case serves to

---

[2] Units of colour difference are defined by the CIE [23] and here we are referring to the CIE *LUV* unit of colour difference.

show that memory for the optimal colour due to familiarity is not a sufficient explanation for the decrease in reading speed with departures from optimal colour.

The extraordinary precision required for optimal reading speed might lead one to suppose that the variation in colour due to differences in lighting might be sufficient to reduce or eliminate any benefit from the tinted lenses. I measured 1000 tints provided using the *Intuitive Colorimeter* system and calculated the colour (chromaticity) that the lenses provided under daylight, fluorescent light, and incandescent light. These calculations suggested that, for most lenses tinted using this system, the variation in colour due to lighting is not so great as to render the tint ineffective under any of the conventional sources of white light. Purple tints provide a possible exception. They are particularly susceptible to variations in the lighting, at least in theory. This is because purple tints transmit light at both short and long ends of the spectrum and absorb light in the middle of the spectrum. They therefore exaggerate the difference between daylight and lights that have most of their energy at long wavelengths such as incandescent lighting. If patients find the glasses ineffective under certain lighting conditions, it is possible to provide a second pair suited to these conditions using the computer program available to optometrists who use the *Intuitive Colorimeter*, see Figure 15.4. This is not usually necessary.

4 Alternative systems

The various systems for precision ophthalmic tinting will be described in the order in which they were developed.

Irlen system

As mentioned in Chapter 2, Irlen was the first to offer a service in which glasses were tinted to an individual's requirement. In the Irlen system, the individual observes text through tinted trial lenses, comparing lenses successively. The trial lenses that improve perception are then combined by placing one upon another. In general these trial lenses are similar in colour (e.g. yellow and orange), and the combination has a colour between the two (e.g. orangey-yellow). Occasionally, however, some component lenses may have colours that are complementary (e.g. yellow and blue). One colour then "cancels the other out" and the result is a dark grey lens. Even if the colours are not strictly complementary, the dyes may counteract each other to a more limited extent, and the combination of dyes may be unnecessarily dark. With this system there is no guarantee that the colour formed by combining the trial lenses will be better than either of the lenses on their own. Further, there is no limit to the number of trial lenses that can be combined. Sometimes many dyes are used, and it may then be difficult to maintain colour control of spectacle lenses because dyes tend to leach out in the tint bath when other dyes are added. No technical data on the Irlen system of trial lenses have been published, so it is not possible to know whether the precision of tints is sufficient, or whether there are regions of the colour map (UCS diagram, see Plate 1) that are not catered for.

Intuitive Colorimeter system

The *Intuitive Colorimeter* is described in detail at the end of this chapter. It is a device that illuminates a page of text with coloured light. The colour can be varied using three controls, one for hue, one for saturation and one for brightness. The hue and saturation controls are continuous – any hue and saturation can be obtained within the range or "gamut" available. The brightness control is discrete: four levels of brightness are available. The instrument has the advantage over the use of trial lenses in that, within a large range, the variation in colour is continuous and any colour can be obtained. It also has the advantage that the effects of the colour can be assessed while the eyes are adapted to that colour. The eyes can take at least a minute to adapt to a coloured light [39], and the adaptation time depends on wavelength [40]. The *Intuitive Colorimeter* is used to obtain a colour that reduces perceptual distortion. The colour is then precisely matched using tinted trial lenses, described in detail in the next chapter. The trial lenses are used to assess the effects of the colour under more natural viewing conditions, and further refinements to the tint can be made if necessary. The combination of trial lenses is used to provide the specification of the tint and constitutes a prescription of the required colour. This prescription is sent to a dyeing company and spectacle lenses are dyed to the appropriate shade, and then ratified by spectroradiometer and computer. Contact lenses can be provided, but are appropriate only when the tint is worn continuously, rather than just for reading. They are not recommended for patients who are too young to have the necessary levels of hygiene.

Chromagen system

Chromagen contact lenses were originally developed by David Harris as an aid for individuals with anomalous colour vision. By providing a tinted contact lens in one eye, patients could be given a binocular cue to help them discriminate colours that otherwise appeared identical. The system consists of eight colours and trial lenses with different saturations. The assessment involves the comparison of trial lenses, sometimes with different colours in each eye.

The data shown in Plate 2 indicates that any system that cannot provide tints to match any chromaticity to within the tolerance of a CIE colour difference of 20 cannot offer optimal therapy. No technical data on the Chromagen system have been published, but it is fair to assume that the Chromagen system cannot provide the required precision because of the limited number of possible lens colours.

5 Differences between overlays and lenses

The colour of an overlay that an individual chooses is rarely the same as the colour of lenses they choose, in fact there is little relationship between the two. The simplest explanation for this would be that individuals are poor at selecting an optimal colour and, as a result, random variation masks the underlying relationship. This explanation is not the case, however [41]. Individuals who had previously been using an overlay successfully and were being considered for coloured lenses were asked to read a passage from the *Rate of Reading Test* with and without their overlays. Unlike lenses, overlays are in contact with the page, and the light has to pass through the overlay once to reach the page and again after reflection from the paper. This increases the saturation of the colour. We made glasses that matched the overlay in colour and allowed for this increase in saturation. The glasses were not as effective as the overlay in increasing the speed of reading. We also made glasses that matched the Colorimeter setting (i.e. the colour of the glasses had been selected while the eyes were adapted to colour). These glasses were just as effective as the overlay in increasing reading speed. One possible reason for these results is that the state of adaptation of the eyes differs for overlays and lenses. Lenses have an effect similar to that of a coloured light: everything within the visual field is coloured, and the eyes adapt to that colour and take account of it. Overlays, on the other hand, provide a surface colour, and are viewed while the eyes are adapted to white light.

6 Common concerns

Do you need the same colour in both eyes?

Some people require spectacle lenses that are not the same strength for both eyes because of different refractive errors. Sometimes there is a pathology that is greater in one eye than the other. Even people with otherwise normal vision sometimes report that colours look different through each eye. In these instances at least, it would seem sensible to use tinted trial lenses to check whether a different tint in each eye might be preferable. There have as yet been no formal studies to determine how this might best be achieved. (We are currently undertaking such a study.) There are three dimensions of colour: hue, saturation, and brightness, and if one wishes to include different colours in each eye this adds a fourth variable! It will be obvious that it is simply impractical to explore the entire range of the four variables in combination. In the absence of any evidence one way or the other, two obvious strategies are available. One is to obtain the optimum first in one eye and then the other, keeping the other eye covered. This strategy would more than double the length of time required for testing because it would then be necessary to repeat the testing a third time with both eyes open to see whether the binocular optimum was better than the two monocular optima used together. A quicker alternative might be to find the binocular optimum in the usual way and then depart from this optimum by varying the hue and saturation in one eye then the other. This assumes that the best combination will require colours that are similar in both eyes. Even this strategy could be quite prolonged. For example, one might increase and decrease the saturation in one eye, then the other; having done this, one might then wish to change the hue in one eye and then the other. There are two directions in which the hue can be changed: clockwise and anticlockwise, see Plate 1 (central image). Having adjusted hue, one might then have to re-adjust saturation, and so on. There is no guarantee that such methods, time-consuming as they are, would necessarily find the optimum.

Another possible alternative strategy is that adopted by David Harris in the Chromagen system. He uses a range of coloured trial lenses over one eye only, finding the optimum with both eyes open. The best colour is then left in place while lenses are placed over the other eye. This technique evolved for the use of monocular lenses in patients with anomalous colour vision, but has been applied in individuals with reading disorders. Harris [42] now reports that most patients in the latter category prefer the same colour in both eyes. It will be clear from the above that the theoretical issues are far from being resolved.

There are also several practical issues concerning the use of different colours in either eye. The intervention is more unnatural. Although we are often exposed to light with different colours, it is only very rarely that the colour differs in both eyes. The intervention is also potentially more invasive. For example, it is important to check that the use of different filters does not adversely interfere with binocular function. This is a real possibility because separate tints might affect the focusing requirements of the eyes differently, and the focusing of the eyes is linked to the way the eyes converge to see near objects.

One obvious practical issue is that the use of different colours in the two eyes makes for rather strange-looking spectacles and tends to limit the therapy to use with contact lenses. These are expensive, and unsuitable for young children.

Does everything look coloured?

Some of you will have had the experience of being outside a house at dusk and looking in at the windows. If the curtains have not yet been drawn and the room lights are on, the interior appears lit with light that has a rather yellow hue in comparison to the light outdoors. The light from filament lamps has very little energy at the short-wavelength end of the spectrum, so the light is indeed very yellow. If you go into the house, the lighting does not appear the slightest bit yellow however. Everything in your visual world is then lit by the same light, and under these circumstances the brain adapts to the colour of the lighting and discounts its effect. This is why surfaces appear a constant colour even when they are lit by light of different colour and shadows are cast across them. The same brain mechanisms of adaptation and colour constancy apply when coloured glasses are worn. Unless the glasses are very strongly coloured, the world appears normally coloured. The brain adjusts to the colour that the glasses provide and allows for this when "calculating" the colour of objects. The rule applies to most everyday scenes except the sky. The sky may be affected by the hue of the glasses, at least for a while. This is partly because the brain is familiar with skies of a wide variety of hues.

In studies that are currently in progress I have asked patients to identify the best examples of red, orange, yellow, green, blue, pink, purple, and brown in a large array of coloured patches, with many shades of different colours. They have done so first when wearing their coloured lenses and then again with the lenses off. For most patients the colour identification is very similar under both conditions.

Road use

Although many patients report finding their coloured glasses helpful in reducing glare when driving or cycling, it is not possible to formally sanction this use. There has been no case law to establish what is and what is not an acceptable use of coloured filters. Many drivers wear sunglasses, but these have colour specifications that prevent their interfering with the perception of traffic signals. When MRC Precision Tints are issued following examination with the *Intuitive Colorimeter* they come with guidance based on the standards for sunglasses, and this guidance indicates whether or not there is a possibility of the tint interfering with traffic signals. Traffic signals can, of course, usually be identified not only by their colour but also by their position, which makes the perception of colour less relevant than it might otherwise be. There is no law preventing those who are colour deficient from driving, although some individuals with red/green deficiency find it difficult driving at night. It is at night that the use of coloured filters carries the greatest risk, although paradoxically, it is at night that the effects of glare are often the greatest. Ultimately it is the responsibility of the user to ensure that their vision is sufficient not only for the legal task of reading a registration plate at the required distance but more generally for safety on the road.

Do you become dependent?

Most individuals wear their glasses for reading and other close tasks. A few wear them all their waking hours. In my view, patients should be free to wear their glasses as and when they find it helpful to do so, without social obligation one way or the other.

Some people find that the glasses help for a while and then their symptoms return. In my experience, this is usually an indication that the tint needs revision. It is then often the case that a different colour will now remove the symptoms. Two cases have come to my attention in which, after several revisions, further revision of the tint was no longer able to remove the symptoms, and the patients were left incapacitated by glare. Fortunately, these patients are rare exceptions. Most patients continue to find their tints useful. Two open trials have followed patients long-term. Both showed that more than 80% of patients were still using their glasses after a year [3, 43].

Some individuals find that the glasses help for a while and then they find they no longer need them. The symptoms no longer occur.

Conclusion

Coloured glasses are more expensive than coloured overlays but they are also more convenient and they can be used for a greater variety of visual tasks. Their use carries a greater intrinsic risk, although experience to date suggests that the actual risk is very low. The colour that is optimal for overlays is not the same as that optimal in lenses.

7 Technical details

What the *Intuitive Colorimeter* is, and how it works

The *Intuitive Colorimeter* is a simple optical device that illuminates a page of text with coloured light. The colour of the light can be varied using separate controls for hue, saturation, and brightness. It is therefore simple to select any desired shade of colour.

A beam of white light from a specially selected set of fluorescent lamps (CIE Type F3) [23] passes through a cylindrical filter assembly (shown in $\frac{3}{4}$ view in Figure 15.1, and as a diagram in cross section in Figure 15.2). The filtered light passes via a square aperture into a viewing chamber with matt white inner surfaces. The filter assembly is divided into seven sectors, each made up of a different filter so as to transmit light of a different colour. The colours of the filters have hues evenly disposed in a circle around white in the CIE 1976 uniform chromaticity scale diagram [23]. Plate 1 (central image) shows the CIE diagram, although the points on this diagram are those of the *Intuitive Overlays*. The chromaticities available in the *Colorimeter* are shown in Figure 15.3.

Patients put their heads close to the viewing aperture so that their entire visual field is coloured with light from the chamber. They look at a page of text mounted on an inner surface of the chamber. The text is formed

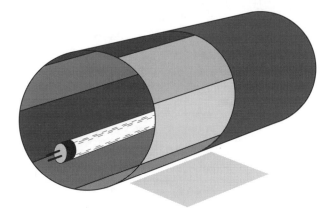

Figure 15.1. Basic mechanism showing filters on the circumference of a cylinder, coloured filters (left) and uniform grey filter (right). The square aperture through which the light passes is shown in Figure 15.2.

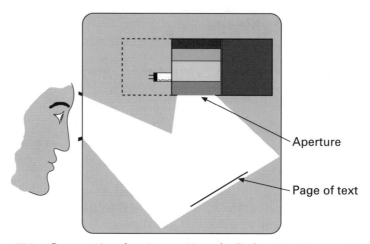

Figure 15.2. Cross section showing position of cylinder at maximum saturation, and (in dotted outline) at minimum saturation.

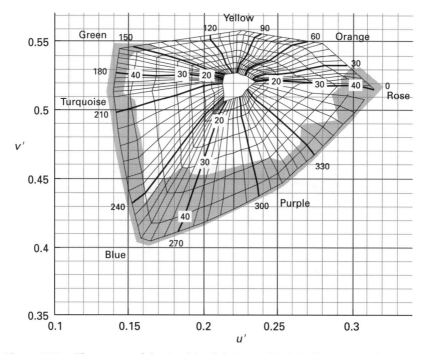

Figure 15.3. The gamut of the *Intuitive Colorimeter* Mark 2. The concentric curves show the change in chromaticity with rotation of the hue control and the spokes show the change when the saturation control is varied.

from randomly ordered letters grouped to resemble words in a paragraph. When the filter cylinder is in its start position (shown by the dotted lines in Figure 15.2) the light is white. When the filter cylinder is slid along its axle (without rotation), the saturation of the colour in the viewing chamber increases, until one or more coloured filters fully cover the aperture. The saturation is then at its maximum. When the cylinder is rotated a filter is combined with one of its neighbours either side, the light passes through the filters, through the aperture and floods the viewing chamber, where the colours are mixed by multiple reflections. The resulting hue depends on the area one filter covers in comparison with the other. By rotating the filter cylinder, combinations of all seven colours result in a continuously variable range of hues. For technical reasons that are discussed elsewhere [44], the spectral properties of the light entering the eyes closely resemble those when Precision Ophthalmic tints are worn under conventional fluorescent lighting.

The *Intuitive Colorimeter* has several advantages for assessing the subjective effects of coloured light:

(1) hue, saturation, and brightness (technically, luminance) can be varied separately and therefore intuitively;
(2) the variation is continuous rather than discrete;
(3) the perceptual effects of colour can be studied while the patient's eyes are colour-adapted;
(4) the assessment is quick and efficient;
(5) the distribution of energy through the spectrum is very similar to that for lenses. The similarity of distributions means that individuals who have a colour deficiency can be examined.

There is one final advantage, and it is a rather technical one. No coloured surfaces are visible within the Colorimeter. It is therefore unnecessary to consider colour constancy mechanisms, at least during the initial assessment in the Colorimeter. Colour constancy helps us see coloured surfaces as having a constant colour despite variation in the colour of the light and shadows falling on them. Coloured surfaces within the field of view have the potential to change the effect of the tint.

Assessment with the *Intuitive Colorimeter*

The patient looks through the viewing aperture of the *Intuitive Colorimeter* at a page of text. The text is lit initially with white light – the same as from conventional white fluorescent lighting (although flicker free). The patient is asked to describe the distortions he sees, and asked the questions described in Chapter 2. The colour is then gradually changed by progressively increasing the saturation, keeping the hue constant. Over about 5 seconds the colour changes from white to a particular shade of rose. The colour remains for a few seconds before the saturation is progressively reduced and the white gradually returns. The patient is asked to judge which illumination was better – the white or the coloured. The instructions emphasise the effect of the colour on the clarity and comfort of the text. The hue is then changed to orange and the orange is gradually increased in saturation and then decreased again. The patient is asked to judge which one was preferable, the white or the colour. Next the hue is again changed by a small amount and the process repeated. Eventually the patient's response to 12 different colours has been assessed, each colour having a hue disposed evenly round a circle centred on white in the CIE UCS chromaticity diagram (see Plate 1, central image).

Usually some of the colours are reported as beneficial, and others as ineffectual or aversive. The aversion is minimised because the saturation of colours has been constrained to moderate levels up to this point in the examination. Now that any aversive colours have been identified, the constraint on saturation is removed. The colorimeter is set to one of the beneficial colours and the patient is asked to adjust the saturation for optimal effect using the full range of saturation. This process is repeated for the other beneficial colours. Having obtained the optimal saturation of each of the beneficial colours, they are then shown successively in pairs, and the patient chooses the most beneficial colour by a process of elimination.

Having obtained an optimal saturation for the best of the 12 colours originally presented, the saturation is held constant, and the hue is altered by small amounts. The patient is shown two very similar hues in succession and asked to choose the best. The chosen optimum is then cross-checked for reliability and consistency. Having ascertained an optimal hue, the patient is again asked to adjust the saturation, this time emphasising the importance of obtaining the minimum saturation necessary for clarity and comfort. Once a suitable setting has been obtained, a computer program is used to calculate the transmission of the glasses that will supply this chosen shade of colour (see Figure 15.4).

The patient is then asked to judge the acceptability of three different levels of brightness (keeping the hue and saturation of the chosen shade unchanged). These are provided using the attenuators on the *Colorimeter*. If the patient is intolerant of low brightness levels, and the computer program indicates that the glasses will be dark, the effects of reduced saturation are assessed at lower brightness levels. If the patient prefers lower brightness levels, these are considered in relation to the darkness of

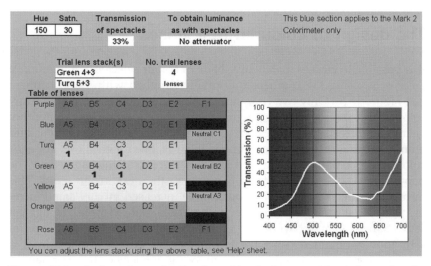

Figure 15.4. A sheet from the Excel workbook that provides information for prescribers.

the glasses. If, as is more usual, the patient is tolerant of a range of brightness levels, glasses are provided with the appropriate shade and the maximum transmission possible.

Coloured trial lenses (see next section) are then made up to match the chosen shade of colour, with the help of a computer program. The program estimates the particular combination of trial lenses necessary to provide a close spectral match to the chosen colour. It provides an indication of whether an ultraviolet blocking dye is necessary, and whether the tint should be worn in the sun. It also indicates how typical of prescribing practice the chosen tint is, and how likely the tint is to affect the recognition of traffic signals. The patient tries out the trial lenses under a variety of light sources and lighting levels. Once an acceptable combination of trial lenses is selected, the tint is ordered, using the chosen trial lenses as the specification for the tint. In the US, a patent by the Irlen organisation may prevent the use of trial lenses.

Note that the Colorimeter assessment differs fundamentally from an assessment with overlays. The test procedure for overlays involves the *simultaneous* comparison of two surface colours, with the eyes adapted to room light. Colorimeter assessment is designed to allow the eyes to adapt to coloured light, and therefore necessarily involves the *successive* comparison of colours. The simultaneous comparison of colours is simpler and suitable for younger children, but is not possible if we wish to assess the effects of coloured light or coloured glasses.

The design of coloured trial lenses

It is possible to closely match any shade of colour selected in the *Intuitive Colorimeter* using the trial lenses normally supplied with the instrument (see Figure 15.5). Only two component colours are necessary to obtain any colour. For example, a yellowy green is produced with a combination of yellow and green trial lenses, and a red with a combination of rose and orange lenses. The lenses are arranged in pairs, one for each eye. For each colour the five pairs are arranged in a series of increasing saturation. The deposition of dye doubles from one pair to the next in the series. This means that the saturation of colour can be increased in very small increments by an efficient combination of the lenses. For example, the lightest saturation is obtained with the lightest pair of lenses. The next level of saturation is obtained using the second pair of lenses. The next level is obtained by a pair formed by superimposing one lens of the first pair on top of one from the second pair. The next level is obtained with the third pair of lenses. The next level after this is obtained with a combination of the third pair with the first. The combinations resemble the 0 and 1 of an ascending series of binary numbers. The five pairs of lenses provide $2^5 = 32$ possible combinations and 32 levels of saturation, or 31 if you exclude the saturation that occurs with no lens! The 31 levels of saturation of one dye can be combined with the 32 levels of lenses from dyes of neighbouring colours, giving a total of $7 \times 32 \times 31 = 6944$ possible combinations of trial lenses, all with slightly different shades of colour, providing close approximations to any possible *Colorimeter* setting, together with many colours that are more saturated than those in the *Colorimeter*.

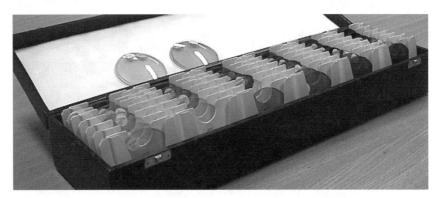

Figure 15.5. The coloured trial lenses supplied with the *Intuitive Colorimeter*.

The lenses were designed with the minimal number of assumptions. It was assumed that it was necessary to be able to approximate any chromaticity very closely (to within one just-noticeable difference). There are many different spectral transmissions that will provide a given chromaticity, see Chapter 6. Dyes were selected from those available so that the transmission was as high as possible and varied with wavelength as smoothly as possible. The purpose of the smoothly varying transmission was to minimise the different colours (metamerism) that result from different types of artificial lighting. Artificial lighting can sometimes have a very uneven distribution of spectral energy, and we wanted to avoid any peaks and troughs in the energy coinciding with peaks and troughs in the transmission of the lenses.

I went to the opticians and got my glasses. I thought they were not actually going to change anything – probably just a waste of time. How would I see different through a different colour? After I came out I tried them on. The first thing that changed was the sky. It was actually blue not a pale yellow. Then I went home and I think I annoyed mum quite a bit asking her whether this McDonald's choc shake was really brown not white as I used to see it . . . Then I went to school and I could read so much better. The words weren't moving around or falling down on a tilt or going up like a hill. There weren't huge gaps and lines missing and I found that as I was reading it properly I could write neater and easier. I don't find reading and writing as hard anymore.

12-year-old girl

After taking part in the trials my life has been totally transformed. I haven't had any visual disturbance, loss of speech, or balance. Of course, like every-one else I still get the odd headache, but not the migraine symptoms I was suffering.

56-year-old woman

James suffers from migraine headaches. He has not had one since he has worn these glasses (5 months). His school work has improved, along with his concentration span.

Parent of 14-year-old boy

sixteen

Why do coloured overlays and lenses work?

> ➤ Pre-receptoral mechanisms
> ➤ Accommodation
> ➤ Photoreceptors
> ➤ Magnocellular deficits
> ➤ Migraine and cortical hyperexcitability

Spectral energy and scattered light

In Chapter 6 the difference between spectral energy and chromaticity was described. It is important to appreciate the difference. Two colours that appear to be the same to the eye and have the same chromaticity do not necessarily contain the same mix of wavelengths. For instance, wavelengths that individually appear red and green when mixed together may appear yellow. This yellow may have exactly the same apparent colour as yellow light that consists solely of wavelengths that appear yellow. The two types of yellow are know as *metamers*. Metamers occur because three classes of cone are equivalently stimulated.

The first colorimeter that I designed provided light with a distribution of energy across the visible spectrum different from that provided by the tinted trial lenses. Nevertheless patients reported beneficial effects when the lenses had the same chromaticity. In other words, patients accepted the metameric match between the Colorimeter and the lenses. It appeared to be the particular relative energy captured by the three classes of cones that was important for treatment. The observation that metameric matches were accepted suggests that the distribution of energy throughout the spectrum is not critical. The observation was important because it greatly simplified the design of the ophthalmic tinting system described in Chapter 15. It could be assumed that it was sufficient to select a particular chromaticity to provide an optimal treatment. This assumption has an implausibility that needs to be borne in mind. It seems intrinsically unlikely that it is *only* the relative energy captured by the cones that is clinically relevant. It may ultimately be demonstrated that the distribution of spectral energy captured by the eye also has its part to play, but until we know more about the physiological mechanisms involved, the simplification that the assumption offers provides a starting point – one that has proved useful.

The eye is shown in cross section in Figure 5.1. An image of the world is brought to focus on the retina but as it passes through the various surfaces within the eye, some of the light is scattered. Short-wavelength light is scattered more than long-wavelength light, and the amount of scatter increases as the eye ages. The scatter might perhaps be responsible for the selection of yellow lenses by elderly patients, because these reduce the amount of short-wavelength light and thereby reduce the amount of scatter. However, this mechanism is pre-receptoral, that is, it relies on effects that occur before the light energy is captured by the photoreceptors. One would therefore expect the distribution of light energy across the spectrum to be critical, and this does not appear to be the case. Moreover, scatter of light cannot account for the range of individual optima selected by young patients.

Accommodation

Short-wavelength light is bent (refracted) by the cornea and lens more than long-wavelength light. As a result, short wavelengths (blue) and long wavelengths (red) cannot both be focused at the same time – when blue light is in focus, red light is blurred and vice versa. The eye usually adjusts so that light in the middle of the visible spectrum (yellowy-green) is in focus on the retina. Short-wavelength light is blurred because it is focused in front of the retina while long-wavelength light is blurred because it would focus behind the retina.

In a healthy adult the lens is adjusting its focus continuously so as to obtain the best compromise possible. If the distance of an object from the eye changes, so will the focus required. The eye takes a little time to make the necessary change of focus, and the focus is not perfect. When the object is very near, the eye tends to under-focus, and when the object is very distant the eye tends to over-focus, as if the focusing mechanism was slightly "lazy". The focusing response is called *accommodation*. It is possible to measure the characteristics of the accommodation using an instrument called an optometer, which shines infrared light into the eye and measures the amount reflected from the retina. Measurements of this kind have been undertaken in young adults with Meares–Irlen syndrome [45]. When the distance of an object is changed, the lens has been found to respond to the normal extent and with normal speed. However, another aspect of the focusing is in fact abnormal. This aspect concerns the fluctuation in focus that occurs continually as the eyes "hunt" for the best focussed image. The fluctuations are abnormally large in people with Meares–Irlen syndrome. This is the only objective sign of any abnormality yet discovered, but unfortunately it does not indicate a cause. The abnormal fluctuations are reduced (but not to normal levels) when the prescribed coloured lenses are worn. The fluctuations are also reduced to an equivalent extent when the individual wears dark lenses or lenses with a colour complementary to that provided in their tint prescription. This lack of colour specificity would seem to suggest that the fluctuations in focusing power are not part of the explanation of the benefit gained from coloured lenses. In other words, the fluctuations are correlated with Meares–Irlen syndrome, but they do not cause it. They may reflect some abnormality elsewhere in the central nervous system and it is this abnormality rather than the abnormality in focusing power that may provide the explanation of the benefits of coloured lenses.

Photoreceptors

Scotopic vision is the name given to vision at low light levels subserved by the rods alone. There is some evidence that the rods are involved in controlling the size of the pupil of the eye as it adjusts to brightness level, even when the brightness levels are quite high and in the (photopic) range where the cones are active [46–48]. The size of the pupil influences the quality of the retinal image in much the same way as the aperture size in a camera – smaller apertures giving sharper images when the light is

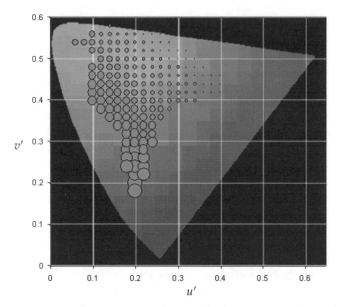

Figure 16.1. Ratio of scotopic to photopic luminous transmission for tinted lenses. The points show the chromaticity of the tinted lenses and the area of individual points is proportional to the scotopic/photopic ratio.

sufficiently bright. In order to see whether any abnormalities in scotopic vision might contribute to Meares–Irlen syndrome, I measured the spectral transmission of a large sample of tints and calculated the proportion of light that would be captured by the rods when the tints were worn (scotopic luminance) and compared it with the proportion captured by the cones (photopic luminance). I assumed daylight conditions. In Figure 16.1, the area of the dots is proportional to the ratio of scotopic to photopic luminance and, as can be seen, the ratio is greater for blue light than for light of other colours. Does this ratio bear any relationship to the choice of colour used for spectacle prescriptions? The distribution of the colours of spectacle prescriptions is shown in Figure 16.2. Each point represents the colour (chromaticity) of a prescription for tinted lenses. There are 1000 prescriptions, and you can see that the majority of prescriptions are either a shade of green or of blue. (The distribution of tint chromaticities is not simply the result of restrictions on the choice of colour within the gamut available using the *Intuitive Colorimeter*,[1] or due to the available combina-

---

[1] The distribution of chromaticities of lenses is very similar for prescriptions issued using the *Intuitive Colorimeter* Mark 1 and the *Intuitive Colorimeter* Mark 2, even though the two instruments differ in the colour gamut available.

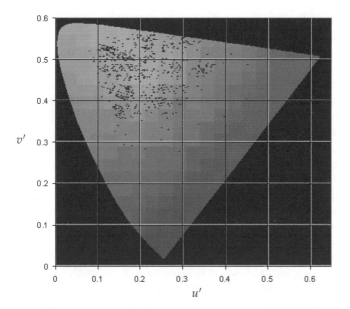

Figure 16.2. Chromaticities of 1000 consecutive prescriptions for Precision Tints.

tions of tinted trial lenses.[2]) There seems to be little relationship between the size of the points in Figure 16.1 and the density of points in Figure 16.2. In other words, it does not appear that the most commonly chosen tints affect the ratio of scotopic to photopic luminance in any consistent way. There is therefore little evidence to support a mechanism for Meares–Irlen syndrome involving the influence of rod function on the size of the pupil. The above conclusion is supported by the following observation. The first design of the *Intuitive Colorimeter* (Mark 1) used filtered light from a filament lamp. This instrument has now been replaced by a second instrument (Mark 2) that uses a fluorescent lamp. The ratio of scotopic energy to photopic energy in the second instrument is only about two-thirds that in the earlier design. This is partly because fluorescent sources are deficient in scotopic energy [47]. Despite the difference in scotopic energy, there is no difference at all in the chromaticities of prescriptions provided using the two instruments. Even though the distributions of these chromaticities show marked clusters, these clusters are remarkably similar for prescriptions provided from both instruments.

[2] There is no correlation between the number of trial lenses required for a prescription and the area of the chromaticity diagram in which the prescriptions are most commonly issued.

The lack of any obvious influence of scotopic energy on the choice of prescriptions is of relevance in another context. Light reception in the vertebrate eye is not confined to rod and cone photoreceptors [17]. The retinal ganglion cells rather than the rods and cones appear to be responsible for receiving the light energy that controls the daily (circadian) rhythms of the body [49], particularly the rhythms of the hormone melatonin. Short-wavelength energy (around 460–470 nm [17, 50] is the most important for keeping the rhythms of melatonin going. This short-wavelength energy is similar to that at which the rods are most sensitive [51]. If light that matches in chromaticity has similar effects in reducing perceptual distortions, as the evidence reviewed in this section would seem to indicate, then it is the energy captured by the cones that is critical, rather than that captured by the rods or even the retinal ganglion cells. As we will see, this does not necessarily mean that the cones operate abnormally in Meares–Irlen syndrome.

The cones operate only at daylight levels. As mentioned earlier, there are three categories of cones distributed throughout the retina: one category sensitive to long wavelengths, one to middle wavelengths and one to short wavelengths.

Some individuals have anomalous colour vision, and the anomaly can be either inherited or acquired. The most common form of inherited colour vision deficiency is caused by a genetic defect on the X chromosome. This produces an altered sensitivity in either the long- or middle-wavelength cones, or else the complete absence of one class of cone. Colour vision anomalies can also result from abnormalities in the short-wavelength cones, although these are rarer and usually the result of disease or trauma. As we saw in Chapter 6, there is nothing to suggest that individuals with Meares–Irlen syndrome are more likely than others to have any anomaly of colour vision, nor is there greater prevalence of colour vision anomalies in the families of individuals with Meares–Irlen syndrome. Deficits in colour vision in clinical tests (other than the Ishihara test [21]) are no more or less prevalent than would be expected on the basis of age and gender [19], as described in Chapter 6.

The long- and middle-wavelength cones are far more numerous than the short-wavelength cones, but there are considerable differences from individual to individual in the relative proportion of long- and medium-wavelength cones, even in individuals whose colour vision is quite normal [52]. Could this difference in cone density be responsible for the individual differences in colour preference? If the individual differences in the colour optimal for reading were due to individual differences in cone density, one would anticipate that individuals who read more quickly under red light would read more slowly under green, and vice versa. Those who read more quickly under blue light should read more slowly under yellow, and vice versa. As we have seen from Plate 2, this is not the case. Indeed, the Macleod–Boynton diagram described at the end of Chapter 6 [24], which is based on colour opponency, does not represent the data in Plate 2 any better than the CIE UCS diagram which is based on perceptible colour differences. The mechanisms seem to be closely tied to the perceptual system rather than to precursors at a lower level of the visual system.

Magnocellular deficits

The photoreceptors are connected to other cells in the retina which compare the output of several photoreceptors and relay information along the optic tract to the brain (see Chapter 6). The optic tract reaches the lateral geniculate nucleus (LGN) (Figure 5.2) in which there are several layers of cells, alternate layers for each eye. The first two layers are called the magnocellular layers because the cells are large. The magnocellular layers form part of a fast pathway that processes rapid changes in the visual scene. The pathway eventually ends up in an area called V5 (Figure 5.2) where the cells respond to movement. The remaining layers of the LGN form part of the slower parvocellular pathway which is thought to be responsible mainly for detailed vision of stable scenes.

A selective impairment of visual function has been identified in individuals with dyslexia [53, 54], and at first this appeared to throw light on the way in which coloured overlays have their effect. The impairment reduces the visibility of rapid changes in the visual world. Because vision for rapid changes is subserved by the magnocellular pathways, the findings suggested a magnocellular deficit. This suggestion was confirmed when abnormalities in the growth of the cells in the magnocellular layers were noted in the brains of six individuals with dyslexia examined post-mortem [55]. Magnocellular cells are thought to receive inputs from long- and medium-wavelength cones, but not short-wavelength cones. Parvocellular cells receive input from all three cone types. As a result of the differences in colour processing between the magnocellular and parvocellular streams, the magnocellular deficit in dyslexia has been widely proposed to provide an explanation for the benefits gained from colour filters. It has even been argued that coloured filters may restore an "imbalance" between the magnocellular and parvocellular pathways. No explanation has been offered for the large individual differences in colour optimal for reading, and precisely what aspects of processing are "balanced" has remained unspecified.

The assumption that the magnocellular deficits in dyslexia are the reason for the beneficial effects of coloured filters has arisen partly because the benefits were first reported in dyslexic individuals. It is now becoming clear, however, that colour has beneficial effects in individuals who do not have dyslexia as well as those who do. As we saw in Chapter 8 and Chapter 15, the proportion of individuals with dyslexia who benefit is not significantly greater than the proportion of non-dyslexic individuals who benefit. It is not parsimonious to argue that the mechanisms that underlie the beneficial effects of colour in dyslexic individuals differ from those in non-dyslexic individuals.

Further evidence against an explanation in terms of magnocellular deficits comes from a study in which we examined a group of individuals who regularly used coloured glasses and benefited from them. We failed to observe deficits on any of the visual tasks thought to be subserved by the magnocellular system [56]. This is consistent with the findings of an earlier study which showed normal flicker perception in children with Meares–Irlen syndrome [19]. Flicker perception is thought to be subserved by the magnocellular system.

In short, magnocellular deficits are not necessarily associated with the beneficial effects of colour filters, and the beneficial effects of colour are not necessarily associated with magnocellular deficits. They therefore seem unlikely to be the origin of Meares–Irlen syndrome.

Binocular vision

The symptoms of visual stress are difficult to distinguish from problems arising when both eyes are poorly coordinated. Deficits in the binocular control of eye movement might be expected to result from magnocellular deficits [57], and some investigators have argued that the benefit from colour is a reflection of binocular dysfunction [58]. We studied the binocular vision of individuals who benefited from using coloured lenses [19, 28]. There was a tendency for slightly poorer performance on certain clinical tests of vision (near point of accommodation and prism vergences). Performance was rarely clinically abnormal on these tests – indeed many children who benefited from overlays had binocular vision that was quite normal [28]. It is possible that the clinical tests are performed poorly by patients because they demand significant visual effort.

For example, the test of near point of accommodation requires the individual to maintain single vision of a target as it approaches the eyes. This requires good perception of the target and maintenance of attention. It is therefore possible that clinical tests for binocular function may give abnormal results because of visual stress rather than poor binocular coordination. It is also possible, however, that colour may influence binocular vision directly. Ts'o and co-workers have reported cells in visual area V2 of monkeys that exhibit a colour selectivity, with a preference for shorter wavelengths, and are tuned to detect differences between the images on the two eyes [59, 60]. "These observations suggest that there are interactions and intermixing of functional properties between the various subcompartments in the stripes of V2" [60].

Cortical hyperexcitability and visual stress

There is an altogether different explanation for the benefit from coloured filters which draws together aspects of visual stress from reading and symptoms experienced by those with photosensitive migraine and epilepsy [2]. Children who benefit from filters are twice as likely to have migraine in the family as those who show no benefit [3]. The children often experience headache or stomach ache that the filters seem to reduce. The cortex is thought to be hyperexcitable in individuals with migraine [61]. This hyperexcitability may explain the susceptibility to photophobia, given that the visual stimuli that provoke photophobia are very similar to those that trigger seizures in patients with photosensitive epilepsy [2]. Gratings that can provoke photosensitive seizures interfere with perception in normal individuals, inducing a variety of distortions: illusions of motion, shape, and colour [62]. The greater the distortions reported by normal observers, the greater the likelihood of the pattern provoking seizures in patients with photosensitive epilepsy [2]. The susceptibility to perceptual distortions is particularly pronounced in individuals with migraine [63, 64]. As mentioned in Chapter 2, there are many curious relationships between perceptual distortions and headaches. We see more distortions on days when we are going to have a headache, up to 24 hours before ([65], Neary and Wilkins, unpublished data). If the headaches are on one side of the head, the distortions predominate to one side of the centre of gaze, i.e. in one *lateral visual field* [10]. This suggests a greater excitability in the cerebral hemisphere to which that visual field projects, see Figure 5.2. If the headaches are preceded by a visual aura and the aura is confined to one lateral visual field, then the distortions predominate in that field between headaches [10]. This connection between the stimuli that provoke distortions and those that provoke epilepsy points to the possibility of there being certain common mechanisms in play. What then, of the distortions experienced by those who benefit from colour?

It is possible that the perceptual distortions seen in the stimuli that can provoke seizures are the result of the inappropriate firing of cortical neurons as a result of a spread of excitation. For example, we may see (apparent) movement in a static pattern because neurons that signal movement are caused to fire inappropriately. Depending upon its layout, text can resemble a pattern of stripes with stressful characteristics, and when it does it can provoke distortions and even seizures, similar to those provoked by stripes [2, 12].

We are able to see things because of the firing of nerve cells in the visual cortex of the brain (and elsewhere). The pattern of cellular activity in the cortex changes as the visual scene changes. It is not unreasonable to infer that changing the colour of a visual stimulus is also likely to alter the pattern of activity. This is because the sensitivity of nerve cells changes with wavelength, and different cells have different sensitivities. Zeki [66, 67] has measured the spectral sensitivity functions of neurons in various visual areas including V3 and V5, cortical areas where most of the cells code for space and movement respectively. He positioned a light with energy in a narrow band of the visible spectrum over the part of the visual field to which the cell responded. When he changed the energy, the cell changed its firing rate, as shown in Figure 16.3 (from Zeki [68]). The curves in Figure 16.3 show large differences between neurons, particularly in the short-wavelength end of the visible spectrum. Similar differences are likely to exist for neurons in other visual areas.

Zeki's recordings were made during brief stimulation of the cells, without allowing for adaptation. If the eyes are continually exposed to light of a given wavelength composition, the photoreceptors adapt. It is possible, indeed likely, that such processes of adaptation will reduce the differences between responsiveness of neurons shown in Figure 16.3. But it seems unlikely that adaptation will act to completely eliminate all the differences, given the size of the differences between cells. It is therefore reasonable to assume that changing the colour of a visual stimulus changes the distribution of cellular activity across the cortex.

Perhaps comfortable colours change the pattern of cellular activity in a particular way. Perhaps they reduce strong excitation in hyperexcitable regions, reducing an inappropriate spread of excitation. If so, this would explain why the perceptual distortions are reduced, why headaches are a common symptom of Meares–Irlen syndrome, why migraine is so

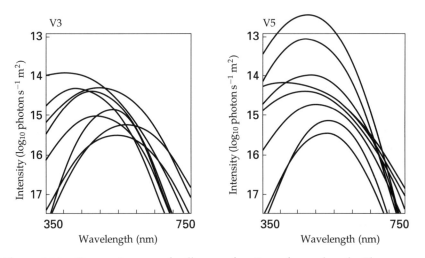

Figure 16.3. Responsiveness of cells as a function of wavelength. The curves show the energy necessary to provoke a response – from cells in visual areas V3 and V5 of a monkey – as a function of wavelength (reproduced by permission of Oxford University Press, from Zeki [68]).

common in the families of children with Meares–Irlen syndrome, and why the headaches remit with the appropriate tint.

Of course, this hypothesis cannot predict which colours should help which people, and the theory is difficult to put to the test. It does, however, make an important prediction: precision tints should be of benefit in a range of central nervous system disorders that involve the visual system and are associated with cortical hyperexcitability. Such disorders include epilepsy, migraine, head injury, and multiple sclerosis. So far, the evidence seems to suggest that precision tints are indeed beneficial in these very disorders. An open trial in photosensitive epilepsy has shown benefits of precision tints in a few cases [69]. A double-masked trial similar to that described in Chapter 2 has recently been conducted in patients with migraine. The study compared two tints, one appropriate and the other sub-optimal, and showed reduced symptoms with the appropriate tint [70, 71]. There are several reports of the visual-perceptual difficulties faced by patients following head injury [72–75], and even one report of a benefit of coloured filters in these patients [76]. I have seen several head-injured patients whose visual function has improved considerably with filters. So far there are only anecdotal reports of success in patients with multiple sclerosis.

The hypothesis of cortical hyperexcitability has found recent support from imaging studies, although these studies are so recent that they have

113

not yet been published. Using functional magnetic resonance imaging (fMRI), Huang, Cooper and Kaufman (in preparation), measured the regional cerebral blood flow in the visual cortex (putative V1) of patients with migraine and matched controls. When the volunteers looked at patterns of stripes, the blood flow increased, and did so particularly for stripes with epileptogenic characteristics, such as that in Plate 3 (Appendix 5). The increase was elevated in the patients with migraine, but mainly in the hemisphere affected by the migraine. This result would be consistent with the hyperexcitability hypothesis.

Although the above speculations may be helpful in predicting the variety of disorders that are candidates for treatment using coloured filters, it will not be until we have a measure that correlates with the optimal colour for reading speed that we will begin to explain the extraordinary effects of colour on reading. So far, the only correlations we have are weak. There is a weak relationship between the chosen colour of an overlay and accommodation, which can be explained simply in terms of the nearer focusing of short-wavelength light, mentioned earlier in this chapter [28]. There is also a tendency for individuals with epilepsy to choose redder colours than individuals with Meares–Irlen syndrome [59]. Neither of these relationships provides any clue as to why the colour necessary for optimal benefit on reading speed should be so precise, nor why it should vary as it does from one individual to another. As shown earlier, the maps that relate reading speed to colour show no obvious colour opponency (Plate 2). In this respect at least they are reminiscent of the map that describes the impaired identification of certain colours in a patient with incomplete colour vision loss [77], or, indeed, the spatially organised representation of colour just discovered in cortical area V2 [78]. Perhaps the hypothesis that colour reduces the effects of a cortical hyperexcitability is valid after all.

Conclusion

The available data suggest cortical mechanisms for the effects of colour on reading and these mechanisms appear to be shared in epilepsy, migraine, and some other neurological disorders. The mechanisms seem to involve cortical hyperexcitability, and the treatment of the adverse effects of such hyperexcitability by so simple a means is a very exciting development. Much more work remains to be done, however, before the processes are properly understood.

On the 31st October 2000 both my sons were prescribed lenses. Joseph is 13 and was diagnosed as having epilepsy at the age of 8. (His epilepsy is now fully controlled.) Around the same time as his first seizure he came home from school and complained that he was having visual disturbances when reading. I had his eyes tested at our local opticians and no problems were discovered with his eyesight. I also mentioned the problems he was having to his consultant and teachers but no-one could offer any help and it was put down to him having epilepsy. He continued to have problems and eventually lost all enjoyment in reading because he found it very difficult. I also began to notice that his spelling was quite poor and his teachers were always telling him to take more care when, for example, copying work from the blackboard.

About a year ago my youngest son came home from school and also complained of visual disturbances. I had his reading tested at school and was told although he was well above average his teacher had noticed that he had to really concentrate and that he did appear to find it difficult when he got halfway down the page. Again I had his eyes tested and it was found that his eyesight was normal. (He has also had 3 seizures in the past which have been unexplained and we have been told he does not have epilepsy.)

Thankfully around this time the school which my eldest attends had a lady from the dyslexic association giving a talk. I went along to this meeting because by now I was beginning to think that their problems could be associated with having dyslexia. After talking to Mrs S and telling her about my sons' problems she told me about overlays and that I could have my sons tested at Hull Royal Infirmary. I went along to our GP and he referred us to the senior orthoptist at Hull Royal. Mrs F tested them both in July and gave them overlays. We then went back at the end of August and she told us about having lenses and referred us to . . .

The overlays had made a big difference to them both but I was concerned that they would not wear lenses. However they were both delighted with the lenses and couldn't wait to show them off at school!

Joseph has told me he now finds reading a pleasure, his writing has improved along with his spelling and he now finds reading and writing a lot easier. He finds it a lot easier when copying work from the blackboard. He is now very happy with his school work and has much more confidence in his abilities. The lenses have made a huge difference to him.

John the youngest has also told me he finds reading a lot easier and feels much more confident.

I am going to write a letter to the Epilepsy Association to tell them about the lenses and how much they have helped my sons because after speaking to other people who have epilepsy, I realise that visual disturbances when reading are very common. I am convinced that a lot more people could benefit from the lenses.

Parent

seventeen

Frequently asked questions

In this chapter we review the questions that people often ask about overlays and try and offer answers. Although many of the questions have already been answered earlier in this book, the following pages may provide a useful summary that can be photocopied for patients or their carers.

1 What are coloured overlays?

Coloured overlays are sheets of translucent or transparent coloured plastic that can be placed over a page of a book so as to colour the text beneath without interfering with its clarity.

2 What do they do?

Coloured overlays reduce the perceptual distortions of text that children sometimes describe. They enable some children to read text more fluently and with less discomfort and fewer headaches. It is important to assess the effects of a wide range of colours because individuals do not all benefit from the same colour.

3 What proportion of children can benefit?

In several studies, children in county primary schools were individually shown a passage of text covered in turn by a variety of coloured overlays, including grey or clear overlays for comparison. About 20% of the children found one or the other of the colours improved the clarity of the text. They continued to use an overlay of that colour, without prompting, for more than three months. They read more quickly with their overlay, both before and after they had become accustomed to its use. 5% of children read more than 25% more quickly with their overlay.

4 How should an overlay be used?

The reader should place the sheet over the page, when reading. The text should be positioned to avoid reflections of light from the surface of the overlay. The overlay should not be creased, and it is a good idea to keep it in an envelope or plastic wallet when it is not in use. Pupils should nevertheless feel free to touch the overlay in order to point when reading. The overlays can be cleaned with a damp cloth.

If teasing is a problem, it may help for staff to explain to the class that the use of overlays to correct sight is similar to the use of glasses. It may also be helpful to trim the overlay so that it is less conspicuous and can be passed off as a bookmark, although it may not then be quite so effective.

5 What are visual perceptual distortions?

Some people can experience distortions when they look at certain materials, particularly text. The distortions of text include blurring, movement of letters, words doubling, shadowy lines, shapes or colours on the page, and flickering. These distortions are characteristic of a condition that some have called Meares–Irlen syndrome, and others Irlen syndrome or scotopic sensitivity syndrome (SSS).

6 How can visual perceptual distortion be spotted?

Visual perceptual distortion should be suspected in children who have trouble learning to read, particularly if they report headaches and eye strain from prolonged exposure to the page. If the child reports any illusory movement of the letters or words, or glare from the white paper, then treatment with coloured overlays or filters should be considered.

One possible question to ask is: "After you have been reading for a while, do the words or letters do anything different?". If open-ended questions such as the above fail to provoke reports of distortions, more direct questions can be given. The child can be shown a page of text, and asked the following questions: "Do the letters stay still or do they move?"; "Are the letters clear or are they blurred (fuzzy)?"; "Is the page too bright, not bright enough, or just about right?"; "Does the page hurt your eyes to look at or is it OK?". Reports of movement, blurring, and glare are more likely in children who benefit from overlays.

7 How are visual perceptual distortions caused?

The cause of the distortions is not known with any certainty. Some authors have hypothesised that the distortions are due to a dysfunction, perhaps a hyperexcitability, of nerve cells in the visual cortex, an area of the brain at the back of the head. Individuals with migraine are particularly susceptible to these distortions and the brain is thought by some doctors to be hyperexcitable in patients with migraine.

8 What is Meares–Irlen syndrome?

Meares–Irlen syndrome is sometimes used to refer to the collection of symptoms and signs of visual fatigue that occur with reading, which are capable of being reduced when colour is used. Other terms are Irlen syndrome or scotopic sensitivity syndrome (SSS). (The syndrome is not yet widely recognised by the medical and scientific communities, and there is no universal agreement on its name.) The symptoms of visual perceptual distortion in children with reading difficulty were first described by Olive Meares, but have been listed by Helen Irlen.

9 What are the symptoms of Meares–Irlen syndrome?

Some of the main symptoms are:

▓ problems associated with glare from the page;
▓ headaches when reading;

- sore eyes when reading;
- movement/blurring of print.

(Onset of symptoms varies and may depend on lighting conditions, style of text, and quality of paper.)

10 What are the signs of Meares-Irlen syndrome?

Some of the signs may be:

- rubbing eyes;
- excessive blinking;
- poor concentration;
- inefficient reading;
- difficulty in keeping place on the page.

These symptoms are not exclusive to Meares–Irlen syndrome.

11 Which texts show a benefit from colour?

Coloured overlays and coloured glasses can reduce distortions and increase the speed of reading, although with conventional text the improvement may only be apparent after ten minutes continuous reading when the child would begin to tire were an overlay not used. If the text is closely spaced, the benefit is more immediate.

12 Which children benefit?

The children who benefit may be good readers, but more often they have difficulty with reading. They usually suffer visual discomfort when reading and, when questioned, will often report perceptual distortions of the text. These distortions usually include apparent movement or blurring of the letters and words. Often there is a family history of migraine.

13 Does visual perceptual distortion relate directly to learning difficulties, or dyslexia?

Individuals with dyslexia may have difficulties with visual perception. These are not necessarily related to Meares–Irlen syndrome. There may also be difficulties of a linguistic nature, which need to be addressed separately. The prevalence of Meares–Irlen syndrome among individuals with dyslexia is not significantly greater than in the general population, despite earlier claims. Nevertheless, children with reading difficulty are slightly more likely than others to report visual perceptual distortion, and to benefit from coloured overlays.

14 Why can children have "perfect eye sight" and still experience distortion?

An optometrist (previously known as an ophthalmic optician) will report "perfect eye sight" when someone can see a letter chart without needing refractive correction (glasses), and when there are no (orthoptic) problems of coordination between the eyes. The perceptual distortions may occur quite independently of any refractive error, although they are often, but not always, associated with a mild binocular vision difficulty (i.e. a difficulty in moving the eyes together, keeping the direction of gaze appropriately coordinated). In most cases the binocular difficulties do not appear to be the basis for the distortions.

15 Does visual perceptual distortion occur in families, and if so, why?

Many traits run in families and visual perceptual distortions are no exception. The genetic contribution is the subject of investigation.

16 Does visual perceptual distortion cause writing to deteriorate?

The visual perceptual distortions that people experience can affect all aspects of visual function, but they are more likely when the visual material has many similar contours (letters). Text is unlike natural scenes in that it is composed of many identical elements. These are at their most confusing in small closely spaced printed text, but they also occur in handwritten work. Writing can be done on coloured paper, and the best colour is usually the same as that of the overlay. The writing is easier for the individual to read if it is double-spaced, i.e. if alternate lines are left blank.

17 Do children need coloured overlays or coloured glasses permanently?

It seems that children benefit most from colour if it is offered as soon as any reading difficulty is suspected, before the cycle of failure has begun. Many 7-year-olds appear to use coloured overlays for a year or two and then discard them as unnecessary. This may be because the acquired familiarity with text makes the distortions less distracting. The need for overlays may return later when intensive study is undertaken.

18 Can overlays or glasses harm the eyes?

Just as some colours are reported as being beneficial, others are often reported to be uncomfortable. Individuals sometimes show a marked aversion to these uncomfortable colours. Provided the appropriate colour is chosen, it seems unlikely that overlays can have any detrimental effect. The possible long-term effects of wearing coloured glasses are unknown at present.

19 Should coloured glasses be worn all the time?

In our view, children should be free to wear the glasses if they find it helpful to do so, but not encouraged to wear them if they would not otherwise do so. The response to colour is subjective and individual, and the wearer is the best person to judge whether there is any benefit. That being said, many children need reminding to do things that are necessary or beneficial for them. Coloured glasses do not necessarily protect the eyes in the way that sunglasses do, so should not be worn in sunlight without discussion with your optometrist.

20 Should children with binocular difficulties who are undergoing orthoptic eye exercises or other medical treatment continue to use overlays?

In our opinion, overlays can be used regardless of any simultaneous eye exercises or medical treatment. However, visual perceptual distortions can sometimes be caused solely by binocular vision problems, so it is sensible to have these corrected first. If the distortions remain then coloured filters need to be tried.

21 How long should overlays be used before coloured glasses are considered?

There are many things to consider. Are the overlays obviously beneficial? If so, only a short trial period, say six weeks, is necessary. If headaches have been reduced, but not eliminated, and if untidy handwriting continues to be a problem, glasses may further reduce the headaches and may well improve the handwriting.

If, on the other hand, the response to overlays is less marked, it seems sensible to see whether the child continues to use overlays without prompting for, say, a school term or longer, before considering purchasing coloured glasses. Coloured glasses are more expensive than overlays, and it may be wise to wait before incurring the cost.

Another factor to consider is the age of the child. It is often difficult to assess a child for coloured glasses below the age of 8, unless the child is unusually mature.

22 Are coloured glasses necessary?

Children who persist in using their overlay usually find coloured glasses more convenient to use. Glasses can help with writing, overlays cannot. The degree of precision in the choice of colour is critical for obtaining the best results, and the precision available with lenses is far greater than with overlays. Perhaps for this reason glasses often give better results.

23 Are glasses the same colour as overlays?

It is essential to realise that the appropriate colour for use in glasses is not the same as that in overlays. For example, a child may choose a yellow overlay and benefit from blue lenses. The colour of the lenses can only be assessed by optometrists or orthoptists who use the *Intuitive Colorimeter*, or by the use of a very large number of coloured trial lenses. Other methods of selecting coloured lenses may be less likely to assist in selecting the optimal colour.

24 Why are glasses a different colour from overlays?

When you wear glasses everything you see is coloured, but you are often unaware of the coloration because you adapt to it and make allowances for it (e.g., the colour of light from a normal household light bulb is very yellow in comparison to daylight, but you are never aware of this). When you use an overlay only part of what you see is coloured and the eyes are adapted to white light. The way that the brain processes what you see in the two circumstances is very different.

25 What is the best method for combining overlays?

The best method is that which most efficiently covers the largest number of possible colours.

The Intuitive Overlays used in recent research were scientifically developed so that similar colours can be combined two at a time in a simple yet thorough way. If these overlays are used and all suggested combinations are tried, a wide range of colours will have been efficiently and systematically sampled.

If a combination of two overlays is chosen, the overlays can be joined together using adhesive tape.

26   How reliable is the choice of overlay colour?

When tested a second time, about half the children in a large group chose the same colour. Half the remainder chose a similar colour (i.e. one with neighbouring chromaticity). Overlay choice is far more limited than the choice of colour in prescription lenses. It would appear that some children vacillate because limited overlay choices do not fully meet their needs.

27   What does one do if a child reports a large range of colours beneficial, but cannot make a consistent choice?

Beneficial colours should be compared side by side. If the choice remains unreliable, then one of the chosen colours should be given a trial for a period of a week, followed by one of the other colours. Alternatively, the Wilkins' *Rate of Reading Test* can be used.

28   Do children change their preferred colour?

Children sometimes seem to change their preferred colour. The precise reason for this is not known.

29   Does it matter if the child still sees areas of white page around the overlay?

Areas of white page may well affect the choice of colour. The conditions of the test should resemble those under which the overlay will be used. If neighbouring white pages are unlikely to be encountered when the overlay is used, they should be avoided during the test procedure.

30   Would it help children to work under lighting that is not fluorescent?

Schools are usually well lit by natural light, and in general, daylight is preferable to artificial light, particularly fluorescent lighting. Care must be taken to avoid glare by shielding work surfaces from direct sunlight.

Complaints of glare from fluorescent lighting should be taken seriously; they usually result from real rather than imagined problems. Fluorescent lighting often emits high frequency invisible flicker that can affect some people. If headaches are attributed to fluorescent lighting, the individual should be seated where the fluorescent light is "diluted" by daylight or the relatively steady light from filament lamps.

31 Can adults be affected?

Yes. Although some people seem to "grow out" of the condition, many do not. The distortions may be less pronounced when reading becomes fluent and text ceases to be a meaningless collection of confusing shapes. Sadly, visual perceptual distortion is often not recognised in children and many sufferers enter adulthood without ever having been treated. There are initial indications that the prevalence of visual perceptual distortions when reading is almost as great in adults as in children.

32 What do I do to find out if colour might help?

First you should obtain an optometric examination. You should find an optometrist, orthoptist, or specialist teacher who has an interest in reading difficulties and uses an Assessment Pack of coloured overlays. Several different packs are on the market with varying numbers of colours.

The pack should include a wide range of colours. It is not adequate to use coloured sheets available from stationers, because there is an insufficient variety of shades.

The examiner should listen to the client's description of the distortions, and use this description when trying to decide whether a particular colour reduces the distortions.

One way of assessing benefit is for the examiner to administer the Wilkins' *Rate of Reading Test*. The test consists of a passage of randomly ordered words that the client is required to read aloud as rapidly and as accurately as possible. The words are all very commonly used and are therefore familiar to most children, even those whose reading is very poor. The words are arranged in random order so that the person cannot guess what words come next. The text is printed in small closely spaced lettering so that any visual difficulty is maximised and affects reading speed after only a short period of reading.

The rate of reading words on this test is usually more than 5% higher with the chosen overlay than without in children who will subsequently make frequent use of their overlay.

33 How can I find an optometrist or orthoptist who has the *Intuitive Colorimeter*?

The company that manufactures the *Intuitive Colorimeter* has a list of optometrists who have purchased the colorimeter. Their telephone number and other useful information is available on the University of Essex helpline (see Question 36).

34 What tests should I expect the optometrist or orthoptist to do?

The precise routine will vary from one optometrist to another but the basic eye test includes refraction (tests of lens focus), acuity (ability to see small objects), tests of the health of the eyes, and basic tests of ocular motor function (how well the eye muscles work together). Children do not have to be able to read in order to take the tests. There are other tests that are not always included in the examination but are generally thought to be particularly important for children with reading difficulties. You can ask an optometrist whether they would do the following tests before you book an appointment:

- Mallett fixation disparity test at near;
- fusional reserves at near;
- accommodative lag;
- coloured overlay testing.

Not all optometrists who have specialised in this subject have an *Intuitive Colorimeter*, but all should know of a colleague who they can refer you to if this further testing is needed.

A standard orthoptic examination will include tests for:

- acuity;
- binocular vision status including fusional reserves;
- accommodation.

Some orthoptic departments may also undertake coloured overlay testing. A few have an *Intuitive Colorimeter*.

35 Will there be a charge for these tests?

The NHS pays optometrists a small fee for carrying out a basic eye examination. As some of the tests listed above are of a specialist nature most optometrists have to charge a private fee for the detailed investigation of people with reading difficulties. The fee varies considerably from one practice to another.

36 Where can I find out more?

The following telephone helpline, courtesy of the University of Essex, has details of where to seek help +44 (0) 1206 872130. Calls are charged at normal rates. The following web site describes research findings; www. essex.ac.uk/psychology/overlays There are links from this site to iOO Sales, Cerium Visual Technologies, and to the Irlen organization.

My youngest son John is now 12. He recently came home from school quite upset as he had forgotten to take his lenses into an exam and unfortunately had found difficulty in reading the questions. He found that he had to read most of the questions several times which was frustrating and time consuming. Later in class he reread the questions with his lenses and realised just what a difference they did make to him ... He told me he has learnt a valuable lesson, and will always make sure he does not forget his lenses again.

Parent

It is interesting that two years on Sarah's eyes seem to have corrected themselves, and she now shows no visible benefit from using her nice green glasses.

Mother of 13-year-old girl

Since I have had the special glasses I can read down the page without having to reread anything twice and I no longer get tired when reading nor do I have headaches as a result of reading. PS. I find them a great asset to my studies as a student nurse.

49-year-old woman

eighteen

Support groups

Where to get help

Support groups for people with Meares–Irlen syndrome have been organised by Liz Ashby of the Norfolk Sensory Support Service and by the Senior Orthoptist, Eye Department, Ayr Hospital. The groups meet occasionally in Norwich and Ayr respectively. An e-group (collective emails) is available from a link on the following web page:

www.essex.ac.uk/psychology/overlays

If you are a patient, carer, or teacher and wish to start a local support group, please contact the e-group, where requests can be distributed to other interested parties.

There is an interest group, called the Colour and Visual Sensitivity Forum, which meets about three times a year, usually in the south of England. The group has participants from the professions of teaching, optometry orthoptics, and psychology, as well as from manufacturers of overlays and tinted lenses. Its purpose is to promote the effective use of colour in the treatment of visual stress. If you would like to join, please contact the group via the web site above.

Parents may find it interesting to read *The Light Barrier* by Rhonda Stone [36], particularly Chapter 15.

nineteen

What the future should bring

The controversial ideas of a German philosopher

The German philosopher, Arthur Schopenhauer, once remarked that each new idea seems to go through three stages. In the first stage it is laughable, in the second stage, controversial, and in the third, self-evident. His was a sardonic backward glance at ideas that have succeeded – many less successful ideas do not get beyond the first of his stages!

The ridicule that greeted the introduction of coloured lenses for reading has now largely abated, at least in the UK. The scientific evidence that this bizarre treatment actually works is now in place. The idea seems to have reached the second stage, that of controversy. The treatment remains controversial because we do not yet understand why it works. Such knowledge would enable us to improve the treatment and target it more effectively. It would also help to dispel the remaining scepticism and controversy and take the idea on to Schopenhauer's third stage.

This book has described the beginning of what is in effect a new medical treatment, a treatment that will doubtless eventually be used in a wide variety of neurological disorders that affect the visual system, including not only migraine and photosensitive epilepsy, but also perhaps head injury, multiple sclerosis, autism, and Parkinson's disease. So far there are only anecdotal reports of success in these latter conditions, but eventually controlled trials will be undertaken and some of these trials will probably reveal benefits that are greater than those of a placebo.

twenty

An epilogue from Sam's mother

"It's been a year now, since Sam first got his green lenses, and the difference is remarkable! He has learnt to use them effectively, does not use them all the time, but plans his reading and his use of the lenses. Sam still visits the library, and borrows books which require different kinds of reading ... for example, novels which he needs to use the lenses for, and graphic novels (where) he can just about see the text in the speech bubbles ... slightly blurred around the edges ... without using the lenses. He still reads quite a lot, more challenging text though ... The lenses have enabled him to improve his learning skills too. He takes much more responsibility for his own learning than he did previously. His reading skills are much improved ... skimming and scanning, searching through text more quickly, and his writing has also improved drastically. Sam's English teacher and I have contact more frequently, he's on the ball and understands Sam's difficulties very well. Sam achieved an E grade overall in the English exam last year, which his teacher, Sam and I were delighted with, because it meant that Sam hadn't panicked in the exam; he was calmer and able to answer the questions more fully than before. One of the questions, he was awarded a B grade for. This surprised everyone except me! Sam uses his lenses for English and History lessons, because the reading texts are longer and contain complex information. For other subjects, Sam occasionally uses the lenses, when HE feels he needs to. They are still as effective now as they were at the beginning. Overall, Sam has made a huge amount of progress over the year, not only academically, but personally. He has become a more confident and happier young man, more assertive, and responsible.

"The lenses have enabled him to become just like everyone else ... to see text, read, decode, encode, proof-read, change, and evaluate his own work – all the things he struggled with before. He's catching up!

"The emotional impact of having the lenses must never be forgotten either. Sam is at the age where image, peer perception, and respect are important, and because his peers can see the difference in Sam's academic abilities and his confidence, he is able to "search" for who he is and be accepted . . . weekend spikey blue hair and all! Sam has come out of his shell, there is a subtle difference that I cannot give a name to, but it is definitely associated with learning about his difficulties, understanding that they are not his fault, and that he is just the same as everyone else.

"Sam's dyslexia and auditory processing difficulties are being ad-dressed too, we are learning how to deal with these all the time, and things are getting better. GCSEs are looming at the end of this year and Sam is concerned about his ability to write enough BUT he is not panick-ing!

"I know that Sam will continue to improve, he has support, people treat him as the bright young man he is. His optician explains to HIM, not me, his teachers are delighted with him, he has very good friends, and of course, Sam's little brother idolises him and wants to be just like him!"

References

1 Irlen, H. (1991) *Reading by the Colors: Overcoming Dyslexia and Other Reading Disabilities through the Irlen Method.* New York: Avery.
2 Wilkins, A.J. (1995) *Visual Stress.* Oxford: Oxford University Press, p. 194.
3 Maclachlan, A., Yale, S., and Wilkins, A.J. (1993) Open trials of precision ophthalmic tinting: 1-year follow-up of 55 patients. *Ophthal. Physiol. Opt.,* **13,** 175–178.
4 Wilkins, A.J., Evans, B.J.W., Brown, J.A., Busby, A.E., Wingfield, A.E., Jeanes, R.J., and Bald, J. (1994) Double-masked placebo-controlled trial of precision spectral filters in children who use coloured overlays. *Ophthal. Physiol. Opt.,* **14**(4), 97–99.
5 Robinson, G.L., and Foreman, P.J. (1999) Scotopic Sensitivity/Irlen Syndrome and the use of coloured filters: A long-term placebo-controlled and masked study of reading achievement and perception of ability. *Perceptual and Motor Skills,* **79,** 467–483.
6 Robinson, G.L., and Foreman, P.J. (1999) Scotopic Sensitivity/Irlen Syndrome and the use of coloured filters: A long-term placebo-controlled study of reading strategies using analysis of miscue. *Perceptual and Motor Skills,* **88,** 35–52.
7 Evans, B.J.W., and Drasdo, N. (1991) Tinted lenses and related therapies for learning disabilities: A review. *Ophthal. Physiol. Opt.,* **11,** 206–217.
8 Tyrrell, R., Holland, K., Dennis, D., and Wilkins, A.J. (1995) Coloured overlays, visual discomfort, visual search and classroom reading. *J. Res. Reading,* **181,** 10–23.
9 Robinson, G.L., and Miles, J. (1987) The use of coloured overlays to improve visual processing: A preliminary survey. *The Exceptional Child,* **341,** 65–67.
10 Wilkins, A.J., Nimmo-Smith, M.I., Tait, A., McManus, C., Della Sala, S., Tilley, A., Arnold, K., Barrie, M., and Scott, S. (1984) A neurological basis for visual discomfort. *Brain,* **107,** 989–1017.
11 Georgeson, M.A. (1976) Psychophysical hallucinations of orientation and spatial frequency. *Perception,* **5,** 99–111.

12 Wilkins, A.J., and Nimmo-Smith, M.I. (1987) The clarity and comfort of printed text. *Ergonomics*, **3012**, 1705–1720.

13 Wilkins, A.J., Lewis, E., Smith, F., and Rowland, E. (2001) Coloured overlays and their benefits for reading. *J. Res. Reading*, **181**, 10–23.

14 Jeanes, R., Busby, A., Martin, J., Lewis, E., Stevenson, N., Pointon, D., and Wilkins, A.J. (1997) Prolonged use of coloured overlays for classroom reading. *Brit. J. Psychol.*, **88**, 531–548.

15 Wilkins, A.J., and Lewis, E. (1999) Coloured overlays, text and texture. *Perception*, **28**, 641–650.

16 Thomson, W.D., and Evans, B. (1999) A new approach to vision screening in schools. *Ophthal. Physiol. Opt.*, **19**, 196–209.

17 Bellingham, J., and Foster, R.G. (2002) Opsins and mammalian photoentrainment. *Cell Tissue Res.*, **309**(1), 57–71.

18 Smith, V.C., and Pokorny, J. (1975) Spectral sensitivity of the foveal cone photopigments between 400 and 500 nm. *Vision Research*, **15**, 161–171.

19 Evans, B.J.W., Wilkins, A.J., Brown, J., Busby, A., Wingfield, A., Jeanes, R., and Bald, J. (1996) A preliminary investigation into the aetiology of Meares–Irlen syndrome. *Ophthal. Physiol. Opt.*, **164**, 286–296.

20 Evans, B.J.W., Wilkins, A.J., Busby, A., and Jeanes, R. (1996) Optometric characteristics of children with reading difficulties who report a benefit from coloured filters, in *John Dalton's Colour Vision Legacy*, D. Garden (ed.). London: Taylor and Francis, pp. 709–715.

21 Ishihara, S. (1970) *Tests for Colour-blindness*. Tokyo: Kanahara Shuppan, 38 plates.

22 Fletcher, R. (1998) *The City University Colour Vision Test*, 3rd edn. Windsor: Keeler.

23 Hunt, R.W.G. (1991) *Measuring Colour*, 2nd edn. Chichester, UK: Ellis Horwood.

24 MacLeod, D.I.A., and Boynton, R.M. (1979) Chromaticity diagram showing cone excitation by stimuli of equal luminance. *J. Opt. Soc. Amer.*, **69**, 1183–1186.

25 Irlen, H. (1983) Successful treatment of learning difficulties. Paper presented at *The Annual Convention of the American Psychological Association, Anaheim, California*.

26 Wilkins, A.J., Jeanes, R.J., Pumfrey, P.D., and Laskier, M. (1996) Rate of Reading Test: Its reliability, and its validity in the assessment of the effects of coloured overlays. *Ophthal. Physiol. Opt.*, **16**, 491–497.

27 Bouldoukian, J., Wilkins, A.J., and Evans, B.J.W. (2002) Randomised control trial of the effect of coloured overlays on the rate of reading of people with specific learning difficulties. *Ophthal. Physiol. Opt.*, **221**, 55–60.

28 Scott, L., McWhinnie, H., Taylor, L., Stevenson, N., Irons, P., Lewis, E., Evans, M., Evans, B., and Wilkins, A. (2002) Coloured overlays in schools: Orthoptic and optometric findings. *Ophthal. Physiol. Opt.*, **22**, 156–165.

29 Kriss, I. (2002) An investigation of the effects of coloured overlays on reading in dyslexics and controls. BSc Thesis, Manchester Metropolitan University, UK.

References _____

30 Evans, B.J.W., and Joseph, F. (2002) The effect of coloured filters on the rate of reading in an adult student population. *Ophthal. Physiol. Opt.* (in press).
31 Hughes, L.E., and Wilkins, A.J. (2002) Typography in children's reading schemes may be suboptimal: Evidence from measures of reading rate. *J. Res. Reading*, **233**, 314–324.
32 Baddeley, A.D., Emslie, H., and Nimmo-Smith, M.I. (1992) *The Speed and Capacity of Language Processing Task: SCOLP.* Bury St Edmunds, UK: Thames Valley Test Company.
33 Mills, E., and Borg, N. (1999) Trends in recommended lighting levels: An international comparison. *J. Illuminating Eng. Soc.*, **28**, 155–163.
34 JCGQ (2002) *Regulations and Guidance relating to Candidates with Particular Requirements.* London: Joint Council for General Qualifications.
35 DfES (2001) *Special Educational Needs Code of Practice.* London: Department for Education and Skills (DfES/581/2001).
36 Stone, R. (2002) *The Light Barrier.* New York: St Martin's Press.
37 British Psychological Society (1999) Dyslexia, literacy and psychological assessment. *Report of a Working Party of the Division of Educational and Child Psychology*, R. Reason (ed.). Leicester, UK: British Psychological Society.
38 Evans, B.J.W. (2001) *Dyslexia and Vision.* London: Whurr Publications.
39 Daugirdiene, A., Kulikowski, J.J., Stanikunas, R., and Vaitkevicius, H. (2002) The effects of adaptation and surround on colour-constancy measurements. *Perception*, **31**(Suppl.), 131.
40 Werner, A., Sharpe, L.T., and Zrenner, E. (2000) Asymmetries in the time-course of chromatic adaptation and the significance of contrast. *Vision Research*, **40**, 1101–1113.
41 Lightstone, A., Lightstone, T., and Wilkins, A.J. (1999) Both coloured overlays and coloured lenses can improve reading fluency, but their optimal chromaticities differ. *Ophthal. Physiol. Opt.*, **914**, 279–285.
42 Harris, D. (2002) Paper read at *The City University Course on Specific Learning Difficulties*.
43 Evans, B.J.W., Lightstone, A., Eperjesi, F., Duffy, J., Speedwell, L., Patel, R., and Wilkins, A.J. (1999) A review of the management of 323 consecutive patients seen in a specific learning difficulties clinic. *Ophthal. Physiol. Opt.*, **196**, 454–466.
44 Wilkins, A.J., and Sihra, N. (2000) A colorizer for use in determining an optimal ophthalmic tint. *Color Res. Appn*, **263**, 246–253.
45 Simmers, A.J., Gray, L.S., and Wilkins, A.J. (2001) The influence of tinted lenses upon ocular accommodation. *Vision Research*, **41**, 1229–1238.
46 Berman, S., Fein, G., and Myers, A. (1996) Luminance-controlled pupil size affects word-reading accuracy. *J. Illuminating Engineering Soc.*, **25**(1), 51–59.
47 Berman, S.M., Fein, G., and Jewett, D.L. (1992) Spectral determinants of steady-state pupil size with full field of view. *J. Illuminating Engineering Soc.*, **21**(2), 3–13.
48 Berman, S.M., Jewett, D.L., and Bullimore, M.A. (1996) Lighting spectral effect on Landolt C performance is enhanced by blur and abolished by mydriasis. *J. Illuminating Engineering Soc.*, **25**(1), 42–50.

49 Berson, D.M., Dunn, F.A., and Takao, M. (2002) Phototransduction by retinal ganglion cells that set the circadian clock. *Science*, **295**(5557), 1070–1073.

50 Thapan, K., Arendt, J., and Skene, D.J. (2001) An action spectrum for melatonin suppression: Evidence for a novel non-rod, non-cone photoreceptor system in humans. *J. Physiol.*, **535**(1), 261–267.

51 Rea, M.S., Bullough, J.D., and Figueiro, M.G. (2001) Human melatonin suppression by light: A case for scotopic efficiency. *J. Neurosci. Lett.*, **299**(1–2), 45–48.

52 Dobkins, K.R., Thiele, A., and Albright, T.D. (2000) Comparison of red–green equiluminance points in humans and macaques: Evidence for different L:M cone ratios between species. *J. Opt. Soc. Am. A. Opt. Image Sci. Vis.*, **173**, 545–556.

53 Lovegrove, W., Martin, F., and Slaghuis, W. (1986) A theoretical and experimental case for a residual deficit in specific reading disability. *Cognitive Neuropsychol.*, **3**, 225–267.

54 Livingstone, M.S., Rosen, G.D., Drislane, F.W., and Galaburda, A.M. (1991) Physiological and anatomical evidence for a magnocellular defect in developmental dyslexia. *Proc. Natl Acad. Sci.*, **88**, 7943–7947.

55 Galaburda, A.M. (1993) Neuroanatomic basis of developmental dyslexia. *Neurol. Clin.*, **111**, 161–173.

56 Simmers, A.J., Bex, P.J., Smith, F.K.H., and Wilkins, A.J. (2001) Spatiotemporal visual function in tinted lens wearers. *Investigative Ophthalmol. Vis. Sci.*, **423**, 879–884.

57 Stein, J. (2001) The magnocellular theory of dyslexia. *Dyslexia*, **71**, 12–36.

58 Scheiman, M., Blaskey, P., Ciner, E.B., Gallaway, M., Parisi, M., Pollack, K., and Selznick, R. (1991) Vision characteristics of individuals identified as Irlen filter candidates. *J. Amer. Optom. Assn*, **61**, 600–605.

59 Ts'o, D.Y., Gilbert, C.D., and Wiesel, T.N. (1991) Orientation selectivity of and interactions between colour and disparity subcompartments in area V2 of Macaque monkey. *Society of Neuroscience Abstracts*, **17**, 1089.

60 Ts'o, D.Y., Roe, A.W., and Gilbert, C.D. (2001) A hierarchy of the functional organisation for colour, form and disparity in primate visual area V2. *Vision Research*, **41**, 1333–1349.

61 Aurora, S.K., and Welch, K.M. (1998) Brain excitability in migraine: Evidence from transcranial magnetic stimulation studies. *Curr. Opin. Neurol.*, **113**(June), 205–209.

62 Chronicle, E.P., and Wilkins, A.J. (1996) Gratings that induce distortions mask superimposed targets. *Perception*, **25**, 661–668.

63 Chronicle, E.P., Wilkins, A.J., and Coleston, D.M. (1995) Thresholds for detection of a target against a background grating suggest visual dysfunction in migraine with aura but not migraine without aura. *Cephalalgia*, **15**, 117–122.

64 Chronicle, E., and Wilkins, A.J. (1991) Colour and visual discomfort in migraineurs. *Lancet*, **338**(8771), 890.

65 Nulty, D., Wilkins, A.J., and Williams, J.M. (1987) Mood, pattern sensitivity and headache: A longitudinal study. *Psychol. Med.*, **17**, 705–713.

66 Zeki, S. (1983) Colour coding in the cerebral cortex: The responses of wavelength-selective and colour-coded cells in monkey visual cortex to changes in wavelength composition. *Neuroscience*, **9**, 767–781.

67 Zeki, S. (1983) Colour coding in the cerebral cortex: The reaction of cells in monkey visual cortex to wavelengths and colours. *Neuroscience*, **9**, 741–776.

68 Zeki, S. (1990) A century of cerebral achromatopsia. *Brain*, **113**(6), 1721–1777.

69 Wilkins, A.J., Baker, A., Amin, D., Smith, S., Bradford, J., Boniface, S., Zaiwalla, Z., Besag, F.M.C., Binnie, C.D., and Fish, D. (1999) Treatment of photosensitive epilepsy using coloured filters. *Seizure*, **8**, 444–449.

70 Evans, B.J.W., Patel, R., and Wilkins, A.J. (2002) Optometric function in visually-sensitive migraine before and after treatment with tinted spectacles. *Ophthal. Physiol. Opt.*, **22**, 130–142.

71 Wilkins, A.J., Patel, R., Adjamian, R., and Evans, B.J.W. (2002) Tinted spectacles and visually sensitive migraine. *Cephalalgia*, **22**(9), 711–719.

72 Bohnen, S., Twijnstra, A., Wijnen, G., and Jolles, J. (1991) Tolerance for light and sound of patients with persistent post-concussional symptoms six months after mild head injury. *Journal of Neurology*, **238**, 443–446.

73 Padula, W.V., Argyris, S., and Ray, J. (1994) Visual evoked potentials (VEP) evaluating treatment for post-trauma vision syndrome (PTVS) in patients with traumatic brain injuries (TBI). *Brain Inj.*, **8**(2), 125–133.

74 Waddell, P.A., and Gronwall, D.M. (1984) Sensitivity to light and sound following minor head injury. *Acta Neurol. Scand.*, **69**, 270–276.

75 Zihl, J. (1988) Sehen, in *Neuropsychologische Rehabilitation*, D.v. Cramon and J. Zihl (eds). Springer: Berlin, pp. 105–131.

76 Jackowski, M.M., Sturr, J.F., Taub, H.A., and Turk, M.A. (1996) Photophobia in patients with traumatic brain injury: Uses of light-filtering lenses to enhance contrast sensitivity and reading rate. *Neurorehabilitation*, **6**, 193–201.

77 Kennard, C., Lawden, M., Morland, A.B., and Ruddock, K.H. (1995) Colour identification and colour constancy are impaired in a patient with incomplete achromatopsia associated with prestriate cortical lesions. *Proc. R. Soc. Lond. B. Biol. Sci.*, **22**(260), 169–175.

78 Xiao, Y., Wang, Y., and Felleman, D.J. (2003) A spatially organised representation of colour in macaque cortical area V2. *Nature*, January 30; **421**(6922), 535–539.

Appendix 1
Test material

The material in this appendix is reproduced by permission of iOO Sales Ltd.

come see the play look up is cat not my and dog for you to the cat up dog and is play come you see for not to look my you for the and not see my play come is look dog cat to up dog to you and play cat up is my not come for the look see play come see cat not look dog is my up the for to and you to not cat for look is my and up come play you see the dog my play see to for you is the look up cat not dog come and look to for my come play the dog see you not cat up and is up come look for the not dog cat you to see is and my play is you dog for not cat my look come and up to play see the see the look dog and not is you come up to my for cat play not up play my is dog you come look for see and to the cat look up come and is my cat not dog you see for to play the my you is look the dog play see not come and to cat for up for the to and you cat is look up my not dog play see come you look see and play to the is cat not come for my up dog come not to play look the and dog see is cat up you for my and is for dog come see the cat up look you play my not to dog you cat to and play for not come up the see look my is the come to up cat my see dog you not look is play and for

come see the play look up is cat not my and dog for you to the cat up dog and is play come you see for not to look my you for the and not see my play come is look dog cat to up dog to you and play cat up is my not come for the look see play come see cat not look dog is my up the for to and you to not cat for look is my and up come play you see the dog my play see to for you is the look up cat not dog come and look to for my come play the dog see you not cat up and is up come look for the not dog cat you to see is and my play is you dog for not cat my look come and up to play see the see the look dog and not is you come up to my for cat play not up play my is dog you come look for see and to the cat look up come and is my cat not dog you see for to play the my you is look the dog play see not come and to cat for up for the to and you cat is look up my not dog play see come you look see and play to the is cat not come for my up dog come not to play look the and dog see is cat up you for my and is for dog come see the cat up look you play my not to dog you cat to and play for not come up the see look my is the come to up cat my see dog you not look is play and for come see the play look up is cat not my and dog for you to the cat up dog and is play come you see for not to look my you for the and not see my play come is look dog cat to up dog to you and play cat up is my not come for the look see play come see cat not look dog is my up the for to and you to not cat for look is my and up come play you see the dog my play see to for you is the look up cat not dog come and look to for my come play the dog see you not cat up and is up come look for the not dog cat you to see is and my play is you dog for not cat my look come and up to play see the see the look dog and not is you come up to my for cat play not up play my is dog you come look for see and to the cat look up come and is my cat not dog you see for to play the my you is look the dog play see not come and to cat for up for the to and you cat is look up my not dog play see come you look see and play to the is cat not come for my up dog come not to play look the and dog see is cat up you for my and is for dog come see the cat up look you play my not to dog you cat to and play for not come up the see look my is the come to up cat my see dog you not look is play and for

come see the play look up is cat not my and dog for you to the cat up dog and is play come you see for not to look my you for the and not see my play come is look dog cat to up dog to you and play cat up is my not come for the look see play come see cat not look dog is my up the for to and you to not cat for look is my and up come play you see the dog my play see to for you is the look up cat not dog come and look to for my come play the dog see you not cat up and is up come look for the not dog cat you to see is and my play is you dog for not cat my look come and up to play see the see the look dog and not is you come up to my for cat play not up play my is dog you come look for see and to the cat look up come and is my cat not dog you see for to play the my you is look the dog play see not come and to cat for up for the to and you cat is look up my not dog play see come you look see and play to the is cat not come for my up dog come not to play look the and dog see is cat up you for my and is for dog come see the cat up look you play my not to dog you cat to and play for not come up the see look my is the come to up cat my see dog you not look is play and for

come see the play look up is cat not my and dog for you to
the cat up dog and is play come you see for not to look my
you for the and not see my play come is look dog cat to up
dog to you and play cat up is my not come for the look see
play come see cat not look dog is my up the for to and you
to not cat for look is my and up come play you see the dog
my play see to for you is the look up cat not dog come and
look to for my come play the dog see you not cat up and is
up come look for the not dog cat you to see is and my play
is you dog for not cat my look come and up to play see the
see the look dog and not is you come up to my for cat play
not up play my is dog you come look for see and to the cat
look up come and is my cat not dog you see for to play the
my you is look the dog play see not come and to cat for up
for the to and you cat is look up my not dog play see come
you look see and play to the is cat not come for my up dog
come not to play look the and dog see is cat up you for my
and is for dog come see the cat up look you play my not to
dog you cat to and play for not come up the see look my is
the come to up cat my see dog you not look is play and for

Make two photocopies of the page and place side by side.

Appendix 2
Overlays Record
Sheet

The material in this appendix is reproduced by permission of iOO Sales Ltd.

Intuitive Overlays Record Sheet

Name : ....

Date : ....

Date of Birth : ....

Male/female

Class : ....

Examiner's initials...............

Symptom Questionnaire

Ask question when individual is looking at text on Test Page.
Response that is __underlined__ scores 1; others score 0.
Enter score in box.

	White page	Single overlay	Double overlay
"Do the letters stay still or do they **move**?"			
"Are the letters clear or are they **blurred**?"			
"Are the words **too close together** or far enough apart?"			
"Is the page **too bright**, not bright enough, or just about right?"			
"Does the page **hurt** your eyes to look at, or is it OK?"			

There is no hard and fast rule relating the above symptoms to benefit from overlays, although, in general, the greater the number of symptoms reported, the greater their reduction with the optimal colour, the more likely it is that the overlay(s) will be used, and the greater the increase in reading speed that results. See Wilkins, A.J. Lewis, E., Smith, F. Rowland, E., Tweedie, W. (2001). Coloured overlays and their benefit for reading. *Journal of Research in Reading*, **24**, 41-64.

Colour of single overlay ....

Colour of double overlay (if needed)................................

You can use this diagram to keep track of the overlays and combinations of overlays you have tested. The colours formed by the single overlays are shown in the inner ring. The colours given in the outer ring are formed by placing one overlay on top of another.

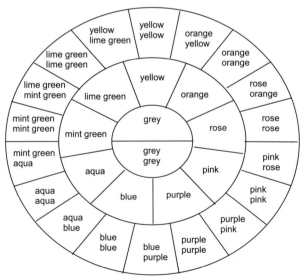

Appendix 3
Rate of Reading Test
Score Sheet

The material in this appendix is reproduced by permission of iOO Sales Ltd.

Rate of Reading Score Sheet

- Hear the passage read once for 30 seconds as practice.
- Hear the passage of text read aloud for one minute with overlay.
- Score using a red pen. Strike out omitted words below. Mark finish thus //.
- Hear the passage read aloud again for one minute, this time without the overlay.
- Score using a blue pen. Strike out omitted words below. Mark finish thus //.

come	see	the	play	look	up	is	cat	not	my	and	dog	for	you	to
1	2	3	4	5	6	7	8	9	10	11	12	13	14	15
the	cat	up	dog	and	is	play	come	you	see	for	not	to	look	my
16	17	18	19	20	21	22	23	24	25	26	27	28	29	30
you	for	the	and	not	see	my	play	come	is	look	dog	cat	to	up
31	32	33	34	35	36	37	38	39	40	41	42	43	44	45
dog	to	you	and	play	cat	up	is	my	not	come	for	the	look	see
46	47	48	49	50	51	52	53	54	55	56	57	58	59	60
play	come	see	cat	not	look	dog	is	my	up	the	for	to	and	you
61	62	63	64	65	66	67	68	69	70	71	72	73	74	75
to	not	cat	for	look	is	my	and	up	come	play	you	see	the	dog
76	77	78	79	80	81	82	83	84	85	86	87	88	89	90
my	play	see	to	for	you	is	the	look	up	cat	not	dog	come	and
91	92	93	94	95	96	97	98	99	100	101	102	103	104	105
look	to	for	my	come	play	the	dog	see	you	not	cat	up	and	is
106	107	108	109	110	111	112	113	114	115	116	117	118	119	120
up	come	look	for	the	not	dog	cat	you	to	see	is	and	my	play
121	122	123	124	125	126	127	128	129	130	131	132	133	134	135
is	you	dog	for	not	cat	my	look	come	and	up	to	play	see	the
136	137	138	139	140	141	142	143	144	145	146	147	148	149	150
see	the	look	dog	and	not	is	you	come	up	to	my	for	cat	play
151	152	153	154	155	156	157	158	159	160	161	162	163	164	165
not	up	play	my	is	dog	you	come	look	for	see	and	to	the	cat
166	167	168	169	170	171	172	173	174	175	176	177	178	179	180
look	up	come	and	is	my	cat	not	dog	you	see	for	to	play	the
181	182	183	184	185	186	187	188	189	190	191	192	193	194	195
my	you	is	look	the	dog	play	see	not	come	and	to	cat	for	up
196	197	198	199	200	201	202	203	204	205	206	207	208	209	210
for	the	to	and	you	cat	is	look	up	my	not	dog	play	see	com
211	212	213	214	215	216	217	218	219	220	221	222	223	224	225

Appendix 4
Group Test
Record Sheet

Group Test Sheet

Name . . . .

Class . . . .

Date . . . .

come see the play look up is cat not my and dog for you to
the cat up dog and is play come you see for not to look my
you for the and not see my play come is look dog cat to up
dog to you and play cat up is my not come for the look see
play come see cat not look dog is my up the for to and you
to not cat for look is my and up come play you see the dog
my play see to for you is the look up cat not dog come and
look to for my come play the dog see you not cat up and is
up come look for the not dog cat you to see is and my play
is you dog for not cat my look come and up to play see the
see the look dog and not is you come up to my for cat play
not up play my is dog you come look for see and to the cat
look up come and is my cat not dog you see for to play the
my you is look the dog play see not come and to cat for up
for the to and you cat is look up my not dog play see come
you look see and play to the is cat not come for my up dog
come not to play look the and dog see is cat up you for my
and is for dog come see the cat up look you play my not to
dog you cat to and play for not come up the see look my is
the come to up cat my see dog you not look is play and for

Look at the text above and then answer these questions by ticking the boxes

1. Do the letters stay still or do they move? stay still ☐ move ☐

2. Are the letters clear or are they blurred? clear ☐ blurred ☐

3. Are the words too close together or far enough apart? too close ☐ far enough apart ☐

4. Is the page too bright, or just about right? too bright ☐ about right ☐

5. Does the page hurt your eyes to look at, or is it OK? hurts eyes ☐ OK ☐

Appendix 5
Plate 3

A stressful pattern of stripes. DO NOT LOOK AT THIS PATTERN IF YOU HAVE EPILEPSY OR MIGRAINE.

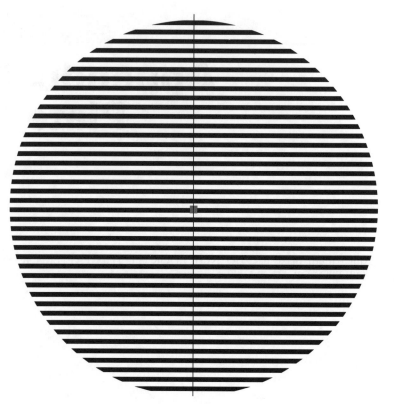

Plate 3. A stressful pattern of stripes. DO NOT LOOK AT THIS PATTERN IF YOU HAVE EPILEPSY OR MIGRAINE.

Index

scotopic sensitivity syndrome *see*
    Meares–Irlen syndrome
scotopic vision 105–8
screening issues 67–70
shades 12, 28, 88, 97
shared books 72
short-wavelength light 104, 108
signs, visual stress 17–18
Sihra, Dr N. 86
silent reading 48–50
sizes, text 48, 56
skies 93
spacing, text 48, 56
Special Educational Needs and
    Disability Act 2001 74–5
spectral energy 103–4
The Speed and Capacity of Language
    Processing Task 49
speed *see* reading speed
Stone, R. 75, 82
strain, eyes 18–19
strategies, reading 45
stripes 8, 112, 150
strong colours 61–3
support groups 130
surfaces 36, 60–1
symptoms
    ADHD 82–3
    dyslexia 82–3
    Meares–Irlen syndrome 68, 82–3
    visual stress 15–17, 44–5

teachers 67–70
technical details, *Intuitive Overlays*
    34–5
Test Pages 56–7, 60–1, 139–42
testimonials 32, 66, 79–80, 84, 102,
    115–16, 129
tests
    see also Rate of Reading Test
    Baddeley Silly Sentences Test 49
    conventional tests 3
    double-masked tests 10–12, 41
    groups 69–70
    overlays 38–40, 43–6, 63–5

procedures 55–65, 69–70
repetitions 65
The Speed and Capacity of
    Language Processing Task 49
time issues 91
text
    children 47–8
    distortions 15–16, 67–8
    sizes 48, 56
    spacing 48, 56
    stripes 8, 112
thin film transistor displays (TFT) 78
time issues 91
Tinter (Hamer) 77
tints 12, 28, 88, 97
traffic signals 93
Ts'o, D.Y. 111
Tyrrell, R. 12–13, 39–40

Uniform Chromaticity Scale (UCS)
    29–31
    see also chromaticities
    assessments 98
    glasses 87
    Intuitive Colorimeter 95
    Intuitive Overlays 345
    photoreceptors 109

visible light 26–7
vision
    binocular vision 110–11
    colours 26–8
    scotopic vision 105–8
    visual cortex 24
    visual pathways 23–5, 109
visual stress 14–19
    binocular vision 110–11
    computers 76, 78
    cortical hyperexcitability 111–14
    historical aspects 8–9
    migraines 17, 19
    overlay tests 39, 44–5
    symptoms 15–17, 44–5